**History in black and white:
an analysis of
South African school
history textbooks**

History in black and white:

an analysis of South African school history textbooks

by Elizabeth Dean,
Paul Hartmann
and May Katzen

Unesco

The authors are responsible for the choice and the presentation of the facts contained in this book and for the opinions expressed therein, which are not necessarily those of Unesco and do not commit the Organization.

Published in 1983 by the United Nations Educational, Scientific and Cultural Organization
7 place de Fontenoy, 75700 Paris
Printed by Duculot, Gembloux

ISBN 92-3-102092-7

© Unesco 1983
Printed in Belgium.

Preface

In 1967 Unesco published *Apartheid: Its Effects on Education, Science, Culture and Information*. A revised and enlarged edition appeared in 1972.

The chapter on information discussed the press, radio and cinema principally in terms of ownership and of those regulations which controlled the flow of certain types of 'news'. It was found then that, at this rather circumscribed level, legislative acts, decisions, juridical regulations and administrative orders restricted information. This restriction, however, was neither arbitrary nor a question of chance.

Censorship was primarily framed so as to prevent the dissemination of certain ideas such as racial equality or the capacity of Africans to construct viable nation-states. Censorship, however, was only part of the story and has to be seen within the framework of the Suppression of Communism Act No. 44 of 1950 and its several amendments. This Act gave such a wide definition of communism that any opposition to apartheid could be defined as 'communism' and therefore come within the terms of the Act. It permitted not only the suppression of publications; people could be served with banning notices and restrictions placed on their activities, including their right to publish or to have access to information.

The area of textbooks was of considerable interest. It could be argued that if censorship of information was principally intended to maintain the system of apartheid, this massive government intervention would be accompanied by a more subtle—and some would argue more effective—slant within those texts which were officially used as part of the process known as socialization. This was indeed found to be so in the Unesco reports of 1967-72. These built in particular on the Auerbach (1965) research published as *The Power of Prejudice in South African Education*.

The present study re-examines and takes further the analysis of South African textbooks and the way in which they reflect the preoccupations of a political system based on racial segregation. The study itself, as Professor J. Halloran indicates in his Foreword, is part of a series that seeks to explore the relationship between the media and society. These studies—*Race as News* (Unesco, 1974) and *Ethnicity and the Media* (Unesco, 1977)—indicate that at least one of the 'roles' of the media is legitimation. If this is so, one would expect that, in apartheid South Africa, legitimation would be reflected in the ways in which school textbooks handle those subjects most obviously linked to an understanding of South African society. Since within South Africa the official ideology is white supremacy, the presentation of groups is likely to portray white dominance, the naturalness of white control and the presumed disasters that would follow majority rule. Majority rule is officially linked to 'communism' and the justification of apartheid has, in some official statements, been represented as the protection of 'Christian' civilization against a 'communist' threat to the security of southern Africa. One would expect this to be reflected in textbooks and curricula either in the form of specific instructions or in the slant of the text.

This study does not deal with the important issue of the way that subjects are actually taught. Obviously, apart from what is in written texts, acceptable behaviour, lines of conflict, patterns of dominance will also be conveyed by the attitudes of techers to the materials they use, the students they teach and to the society itself. Besides this the apartheid ideology will be transmitted by the actual situations in which children live and play or in which their parents work.

The present situation, briefly described at the beginning of this particular study, needs to be underlined. South Africa is the only country in the world which officially proclaims racism as its state ideology and racial segregation in all spheres of life as its official policy. South Africa has proceeded to implement this policy in the face of massive black protest within its borders, and the protests of the international community beyond.

While, therefore, Unesco has commissioned this study within the framework of an intellectual freedom the Republic of South Africa itself denies, it is in no way neutral on the question of apartheid. Indeed the constitution of Unesco places on it specific duties with regard to peace, to human rights and to ending racism, and this book is published as a contribution to the understanding of the social mechanisms that support apartheid.

Contents

Foreword, *9*

Definitions, *11*

1. Introduction and background to the study, *13*
2. Education in South Africa—a profile, *21*
3. Aims and methods of textbook analysis, *37*
4. The distribution of subject-matter, *45*
5. Black and white in the early nineteenth century, *52*
6. South African contemporary history, *65*
7. Social and political change in Africa, *84*
8. Conclusions, *102*

Appendices, *107*

References, *135*

Foreword

Professor James D. Halloran,
Director,
Centre for Mass Communication
Research,
University of Leicester;
President,
International Association for Mass
Communication Research

The Centre for Mass Communication Research at the University of Leicester, which is the headquarters of the International Association for Mass Communication Research, was established in 1966 to carry out research on media institutions and on all aspects of the communication process. This would be done not in isolation, but in relation to other processes and institutions, at national and international levels.

From the outset a policy and problem-oriented approach was pursued which, put simply, was characterized by attempts to ascertain how the media were operating, and how they might possibly operate, in relation to important social issues.

It is not surprising, therefore, that from its very early days the centre developed a co-operative working relationship with Unesco—a relationship that led to research, policy formulation and several publications.

In a broad sense the research reported in two of these publications—*Race as News* (Unesco, 1974) and *Ethnicity and the Media* (Unesco, 1977)—may be seen as the forerunner of the research reported in these pages, research that demonstrates a continuing concern in the vitally important area of race and communications.

This textbook project, then, should not be seen in isolation, but as an integral part of an ongoing programme. Although well worth while in its own right, this work was seen from the beginning as a small-scale, short-term study—with the resources available the limitations were inevitable—intended to pave the way for a more thoroughgoing, comprehensive study at a later date. In fact, this follow-up study has now started, and in the course of it the textbook analysis will be extended to other countries, and some aspects of popular literature will also be included.

This whole programme owes much to the concern, insight and initiative of Marion O'Callaghan, and I am most grateful to her and to my colleagues at the Centre for Mass Communication Research at Leicester, Elizabeth Dean, Paul Hartman and May Katzen, who carried out the research and prepared this report.

I am also pleased to join the authors in thanking the very many people in universities, training colleges and other institutions, both in the Republic of South Africa and the United Kingdom, who gave of their time and experience in the course of this research. Dr F. E. Auerbach and Mr E. Viglieno were particularly helpful.

Definitions

A good deal of confusion and controversy surrounds the use of terms to describe the different population groups in South Africa. It is necessary therefore at the outset to give some brief definitions of official and popular usage of terms, as well as defining our own terminology in this study.

African: This term is sometimes used to describe the indigenous black population of South Africa. We have in general used the word *black* to describe this group in the South African context. However, since our study is also concerned with aspects of history elsewhere on the African continent, we have used the word *African* to denote the black populations of other African countries.

Afrikaner: This term is used to describe that section of the white population of South Africa who are mainly descended from the original Dutch, German and French settlers, and who speak the Afrikaans langage. While we have used this term in this study, we have also sometimes used the older term *Boer* (which translates as 'farmer' in Afrikaans) to refer to the Afrikaner group, particularly before the twentieth century.

Asian: This is the official classification for the group which originated from the Indian subcontinent and were brought to South Africa as indentured labourers in the nineteenth century, as well as the significantly smaller Chinese group in South Africa. We have tended to use the word *Indian* rather than *Asian* to describe this group.

Bantu: This is in fact a linguistic term referring to a group of indigenous languages and was formerly applied as an official classification to the black group in South Africa who speak these languages. The official term is now *black*, although we have frequently encountered the term *Bantu* in history textbooks.

Black: As noted above, this term is used to describe the Bantu-speaking black population of South Africa. The term *black* is also used by supporters of the 'Black Consciousness' movement to include the coloured and Indian groups in South Africa. However, in order to avoid confusion we have tended to refer to each group separately as the textbooks do or, on occasion, to use the term *non-white* as a shorthand way of referring to all these groups collectively.

Bushmen: This term is used in the history textbooks to describe the indigenous groups of hunter-gatherers who inhabited the Cape when the early white settlers arrived. The preferred term is now *San*.

Coloured: This term is used officially to classify the people of racially mixed origin who are descended from the Khoisan (Hottentot and Bushmen) people, Malay slaves, black groups and whites.

English-speaking whites: This term refers to the white group in South Africa whose mother-tongue is English. They are also occasionally referred to as *British* in history textbooks. Although this group is mainly composed of people of British ancestry, it also includes people of other European origins who have largely been assimilated into the English-speaking community.

Hottentot: This term is used in the textbooks to refer to the indigenous herding communities who inhabited the Cape when the white settlers arrived. The word *Hottentot* was used by the settlers to describe them. The preferred term is now *Khoikhoi* or *Khoi*. The Khoi and San groups are now collectively termed *Khoisan*.

Indian: We have used this term in preference to the official classification of *Asian* to describe this group. For details on the origins and composition of the group, refer to *Asian* in this glossary.

Whites: The term is used collectively to describe the English-speaking and Afrikaans-speaking white groups in South Africa. Until 1971 they were referred to as *Europeans* in official texts, and this term is still occasionally found in the textbooks.

1 Introduction and background to the study

This is a study of history textbooks used in South African secondary schools. Its full implications can only be seen, however, if it is set squarely within the context of contemporary South African society where a small white minority has access to political power and economic privilege, while over four-fifths of the population are disenfranchised and economically disadvantaged. This manifestly unequal system is based on a person's skin colour, with racial inequality formally enshrined in the South African constitution. Laws define the freedoms and entitlements of every member of society, ranging from where he or she may live, work and play to the type of education that children will receive.

All societies operate through some form of social control. Direct forms of control are found in the legal system of a country, which in turn ultimately rests on the use of force. Such controls operate alongside the dominant values and belief systems of the society, which help to sustain the given social order. Education is one institution through which children acquire socially approved values and attitudes, and textbooks (as a medium of instruction) are capable of both reflecting and transmitting dominant social values. The study of history is a particularly potent means of transmitting values, especially where the interpretation of past events is used to give meaning to the present. Clearly, there may be many interpretations of history, which ought not to be thought of as a body of permanent truths. None the less, history can be, and frequently is, used throughout the world to justify particular forms of social structure and government. South Africa is no exception.

Apartheid and its consequences

The philosophy and practice of apartheid embody the central values of the South African state. *Apartheid* is an Afrikaans word meaning 'separation' or 'setting apart'. It was adopted as the main platform of the (Afrikaner) National Party which came to power in 1948, dedicated to preserving white supremacy. In practical terms, apartheid has meant the systematic separation of South Africa's population along racial lines, thereby formalizing and extending the prevailing system of racial inequality.

Segregation between white and black groups existed long before the advent of apartheid. A form of segregation was introduced from the time the first European settlers arrived at the Cape in 1652, and encountered the indigenous Khoisan people. As white settlement expanded from Cape Town into the interior during the eighteenth and nineteenth centuries the settlers encountered and clashed with the Bantu-speaking black groups, who became increasingly displaced in the face of white expansion. During the nineteenth century laws were passed depriving Africans of legal rights to land and 'native reserves' were established. Controls on the movement, settlement and economic activity of black people were further consolidated during the twentieth century so that by the time the National Party came to power in 1948 the practice of racial segregation and discrimination was well entrenched.

Apartheid is not only a system of racial separation; it serves the needs of the white economy. The creation of 'native reserves' severely limited the land and resources available to black people and, coupled with the imposition of taxes, forced them to seek cash employment in white enterprises. This system was to the direct advantage of white employers who, partly through a process of recruiting black migrant labour and by barring men from bringing their families to the place of employment, were able to keep wages to a minimum—a system which continues today.

As the South African economy expanded during the mid-nineteenth century a degree of black urbanization occurred which accelerated during the twentieth century. At the same time, impoverished rural white Afrikaners were also migrating to the cities where they competed with urban blacks in the labour market. In response to this situation, a complex body of legislation was introduced over the years to protect white workers. This legislation ensured that white workers were given preferential treatment through a system of 'job reservation' whereby skilled work was reserved for whites.

Despite measures introduced to curb it, black urbanization increased with South Africa's economic growth and was used as a rallying cry by the National Party in the 1948 election. The perceived threat to white supremacy from the numerically dominant black group was magnified by events occurring elsewhere on the African continent. The advent of black nationalism, independence movements and eventual decolonization elsewhere in Africa brought the spectre of black majority rule ever closer to South Africa's borders. South Africa's white leaders, through policies of apartheid, have attempted to contain black political aspirations by creating a number of separate 'black states' within South Africa, while at the same time preserving white economic privilege.

The emphasis on separation of 'races' enshrined in apartheid policy extends to all population groups in South Africa. For example, the Population Registration Act of 1950, with its later amendments, provides for the classification of South Africa's population into four main groups: white, black, Asian (Indian) and coloured. Each group has been systematically segregated, and their respective political, economic and social rights rigidly defined.

Geopolitical structure

Geographically, South Africa is considered by the proponents of apartheid as divided into separate black and white territories. 'White' South Africa consists of four provinces—the Transvaal, the Orange Free State, Natal and the Cape Province. (The Transvaal and the Orange Free State were originally Boer republics, and Natal and the Cape Province were British colonies, which were united in 1910 as the Union of South Africa, a dominion within the British Empire, which became a member of the British Commonwealth in 1931. In 1961, South Africa became a republic and withdrew from the Commonwealth.) Within so-called 'white' South Africa, only white citizens hold the franchise and enjoy the benefits of a prosperous economy based on low non-white wages.

The apex of apartheid policy has been the creation of a number of so-called 'black states', 'homelands' or 'Bantustans' within South Africa's national boundaries. These 'black states' have been created partly around the former 'native reserves' and are intended to accommodate each of South Africa's main linguistic black groups. The ultimate objective is that these 'black states' will eventually include all black South Africans and become 'independent republics' with limited sovereignty which will form a federation with 'white' South Africa. Four 'black states'—Transkei, Bophutatswana, Venda and most recently Ciskei—have already been made 'independent'. It should be stressed that this process has met with much opposition from black people within South Africa and that these 'republics' are not recognized by the rest of the world.

Two distinct contradictions arise out of this structure of so-called black states. First, these territories together comprise only 14 per cent of the total land area of South Africa and are incapable of supporting the black population, which accounts for more than 70 per cent of South Africa's total population. Secondly, the South African economy continues to be totally dependent on black labour. In fact there is a growing demand for skilled as well as unskilled non-white labour as the economy expands. Thus the objective of separate black and white nations seems totally unviable. Rather, the independent homelands, like the reserves, seem destined merely to be reservoirs of black labour for the South African economy, while no longer constituting a burden on either the exchequer or the conscience of white South Africa.

More than 50 per cent of the black population resides in white South Africa (see Appendix 1). Here they are regarded as 'visitors', having no voting rights and subject to forced 'repatriation' to 'homelands' with which they may have no direct association. At greatest risk of deportation are those black people who have been assigned citizenship of an 'independent' homeland and who have thereby automatically been deprived of their rights of South African citizenship, as well as those black people who are considered to be superfluous to the white economy. In white areas, black people live in specially designated townships such as Soweto, or in accommodation provided by employers at the workplace from which families are normally excluded. Strict controls are placed on the movement of black people into, and within, white areas through a system of pass laws. All black people are required to carry a 'reference book' (or pass) which contains details about the holder. Failure to produce the reference book on demand is a criminal offence.

Also residing and working in white South Africa are the other two non-white population groups—Indians and coloureds. These groups, like the blacks, live in strictly defined geographical locations. Under the Group Areas Acts of 1950 and 1957 (and subsequent amendments) areas have been set aside for the exclusive occupation of the different population groups. In practical terms this has meant mass eviction and resettlement of people to enforce segregation.

Like blacks, Indian and coloured people do not have the vote in white South Africa. Special councils have been established by the South African Government to represent these two groups and to advise on policy related to them. Despite the appearance of some measure of political autonomy in this system, overall political power is still retained by the South African Government. It should also be noted that these councils are by no means universally recognized by the people they are intended to serve. This is particularly so in the case of coloured people.

Population and wealth in South Africa

South African society is characterized by manifest inequality between groups. The whites constitute only one-sixth of the total population, as Table 1 shows, but they control a disproportionate share of the wealth of the country. As an indicator of the relative disparity in wealth, Table 2 shows average earnings for 1976.

TABLE 1. Trends in population growth (in thousands)

Population group	1970		1976	
	Number (thousands)	%	Number (thousands)	%
Black	15 058	70.2	18 629	71.3
White	3 751	17.5	4 320	16.5
Coloured	2 018	9.4	2 434	9.3
Indian	620	2.9	746	2.9

Sources: 1970 census figures; 1976 estimate, Dept of Statistics, Pretoria, 1977.

TABLE 2. Average earnings in non-agricultural sectors, 1976[1]

Group	Average earnings (rand)	Index
White	5 890	100
Indian	2 336	40
Coloured	1 909	32
Black	1 278	22

1. Excludes private services of legal practitioners and earnings in kind.
Source: SAIRR, 1981, p. 86.

In 1976 the average white wage earner received nearly five times as much as a black, and two to three times as much as a coloured or Indian. The table tends to understate the differences between the groups. For example, the figures exclude agricultural wages, which are likely to be lower than the average given for non-whites. Moreover, statistics on earnings do not reflect the control of assets or access to services such as health, education and welfare, which differ considerably between groups, particularly between black and white.

History as a legitimation for apartheid

Apartheid is not only a set of policies designed to maintain white political and economic domination; it is also a political philosophy which underpins these policies. The ideological origins of apartheid are complex and need not be pursued here. In part they derive from a sense of superiority on the part of whites as well as from the growth of Afrikaner nationalism, which emphasized the importance of cultural identity and racial separation. What is of particular relevance to this study is the extent to which historical explanation has been used to justify the present system of racial separation.

One of the most common myths perpetuated by apologists of the apartheid state is that when the first European settlers arrived at the Cape, the territory that constitutes present-day South Africa was inhabited by only a small number of indigenous people, the Khoisan (Hottentots and Bushmen). In this view, the black Bantu-speaking people who form the overwhelming majority of South Africa's population were migrating southwards at the same time as the white stockbreeding farmers were extending their territorial settlement north and east. Thus it is argued that whites have as valid a claim to this territory as blacks. There is overwhelming historical evidence, however, that black Bantu-speaking people had inhabited areas of present-day South Africa long before the European settlers arrived (see, for example, Marks, 1980).

In using history as a justification for present apartheid policies apologists for the system attempt to persuade the uninformed that separation of racial groups was and is a natural state of affairs. In this context, the *Official Yearbook of the Republic of the South Africa* (South Africa, 1979, p. 208) states:

Over the centuries the various Black peoples settled in different regions where they evolved their own social and cultural systems and tribal organizations. It was only 120 years after the first White men settled in South Africa that there was any appreciable contact between Black and White. From this settlement pattern it followed naturally that relations between the various peoples of South Africa would from the beginning be regulated on the basis of separate and parallel institutions, separate land ownership, distinctive traditions, cultures, languages, as well as on the basis of differing stages of socio-economic development.

History is again invoked in support of apartheid policies in the same publication (p. 203) where the reader is told:

In the light of the country's multinational and historical realities, the majority of Whites are convinced that relations between the White nation of the RSA [Republic of South Africa] and the various Black peoples within the borders of present day South Africa cannot be satisfactorily regulated in a single integrated superstate but rather on the historically tried basis of separate nation states, i.e. a system of political independence coupled with economic independence. This policy—evolved from a philosophy forged and determined by the realities of more than three centuries—has in both official and common parlance become known as separate development or multinational development.

Until fairly recently, a historical paradigm, which makes the assumption that the history of South Africa began with white settlement, held almost undisputed sway. Thus interpretations have tended to present South African history predominantly from a white point of view. Only in the past few years have any attempts been made to write history from a black point of view (see, for example, Marks and Atmore, 1980).

While the dominant paradigm has stressed the role of white groups in history, a distinction must be made between the white groups themselves. In the nineteenth and early twentieth century history was presented from a British point of view and the other white group—the Afrikaners—were denigrated or their role underplayed. Towards the end of the nineteenth century, Afrikaners reacted against this interpretation, and in parallel with the rise of political consciousness among the Afrikaners, a concerted attempt was made to counteract the British version and to develop a distinctive Afrikaner perspective. This perspective has been epitomized in what van Jaarsveld has termed 'the Afrikaner's interpretation of South African history' (van Jaarsveld, 1964).

The Afrikaner interpretation of history stresses the role of Afrikaner heroes and events such as the Great Trek and Anglo-Boer War. Within this interpretation other groups are treated peripherally. A number of myths have grown out of this writing which have been perpetuated to the present day, and which seek to explain the origins of racial segregation and the policy of apartheid. This approach to history has become increasingly influential in South Africa over the years and is exemplified in the historical references in the excerpts from the South African *Official Yearbook* quoted above.

Aims of the present study

The aims of the study are to examine the way that different ethnic groups are presented in South African school history textbooks. Special attention is paid to the extent and nature of ethnic stereotyping in the texts and the endorsement of particular social and political attitudes relevant to the contemporary circumstances of South Africa. The overall objective is to assess how far and in what way these texts form part of the legitimation process in South Africa.

Conceptual framework

A key concept in the research is that of legitimation, which may be loosely defined as the process by which consent is secured among members of a society to the existing social and political arrangements. This is closely related to the sociological concept of 'ideology' (sociological usage of this term differs somewhat from popular usage). The application of these concepts may be briefly illustrated.

In material terms white supremacy in South Africa means that the whites control the wealth of the country, and they also have the guns. For such a system of domination to be viable and lasting it is necessary that the dominant group should maintain ascendancy in the symbolic sphere as well; that is, the exercise of economic and other power needs to be backed by an appropriate ideology. It is important for those who benefit most from these arrangements that they should be widely accepted as legitimate throughout the society. From the point of view of the dominant group it is desirable that as many members as possible of subordinate groups should at least acquiesce in their position in society. Ideally the latter should regard their subordinate status as inevitable, natural, even God-given. This reduces the need to use coercive means to secure their compliance. In order to sustain existing patterns of wealth and privilege, furthermore, a dominant élite needs to be able to count on the enthusiastic support of a proportion of the members of its own group in any conflict with subordinate groups, and the acquiescence of most of the rest. Those with power, therefore, characteristically tend to encourage beliefs and outlooks favourable to the prevailing social order, and to discourage any that threaten to undermine it. This may occur in spite of efforts by governments and others to reverse the trend.

In practice, popular consciousness is cultivated in varied and diffuse ways—through the values transmitted in the home, through churches, schools, the armed forces, the press, broadcasting, entertainment and other institutions. These may all play an ideological role to the extent that the beliefs and values they foster, or the world-views they help to cultivate, promote the endorsement of prevailing patterns of inequality. This is not to say that such institutions are all the same in their cultural impact, nor that there might not be important value differences among them, only that the major institutions of any society are typically the main means by which a dominant ideology is propagated, whether or not they are under direct political control and whatever form any such control or regulation might take.

It is from this point of view that we have approached the analysis of textbooks in use in South Africa. History is an account of past events, and one of its uses is to make sense of the present. People's perceptions of their present-day world are conditioned by their understanding of what has gone before. Different versions of history can lead to different interpretations of the present. In examining the content of school texts our primary interest has not been in their psychological impact on individual readers nor in the individual reasons why readers' responses might differ from one another. Our focus is cultural rather than psychological. Our main concern is with the potential of history teaching to shape the consciousness of whole generations by providing them with a set of shared concepts and understandings about the past that may then form the basis of collectively taken-for-granted assumptions about present-day society and politics. School history may be ideological in so far as it offers an understanding of the world favourable to the continuation of white supremacy and the policy of apartheid. From what has been said above it should also be clear that we do not see the ideological role of history teaching as an isolated phenomenon, but as one among many interlocking institutionalized cultural forces in South African society.

Like other ideologies, the ideology of white supremacy is not something that can be reduced to a set of neat propositions which can then be subjected to definitive scholarly examination. For the importance of an ideological statement lies not in its truth or falsity, but in the function it serves in justifying particular social arrangements. As a matter of fact, demonstrably true statements make better ideology than falsehoods because their legitimating power is more difficult to undermine. What is important about an ideological statement is that it should be convincing to those who need to be convinced. It is the use to which it can be put that gives a statement its ideological character. From the point of view of ideological efficacy it matters little whether it is claimed that apartheid is necessary because blacks are congenitally inferior to whites, or merely culturally inferior, so long as the idea can be made to serve the purpose of justifying the policies of white supremacy. The ideology of apartheid has many variants which command varying degrees of credibility in different sections of the South African population at different times. Theologically based versions still enjoy endorsement among sections of the white Afrikaner population ('It is ordained by God that the races should not mix'), while English-speakers are more likely to embrace explanations of the status quo that stress cultural factors ('The blacks need time to catch up'). Similarly, though it used to be common for official pronouncements to be couched in terms of racial inferiority of the blacks, it is more common today to refer to the difference between the various population groups and their distinctive national destinies. Having said this it remains true that the twin notions of white superiority and the need to maintain separation between the races are at the very heart of the ideology that justifies the prevailing pattern of inequality in the country, and it is with this in mind that our analysis of history textbooks has been carried out.

We approach this study then from a sociological perspective rather than a historical or educational one. In this respect we are less concerned with the historical accuracy or pedagogic merit of textbooks than with the kind of 'world-views' being offered and their implications for the society as a whole.

2 Education in South Africa— a profile

Introduction

This chapter gives an overview of the education system in South Africa as a background to our analysis of textbooks. It includes a brief summary of the history of education; an outline of the administrative structure and organization of education; figures and trends in school enrolment; and information on the curriculum, syllabuses and examination structure. Special attention is paid to education in the Transvaal since this province forms the main focus of our study.

Before examining these specific aspects of education, a few points need to be made about the overall structure of education in South Africa. The first is that, in common with other socio-political institutions, education is governed by the laws of apartheid and thus schools at all levels are segregated along racial lines.[1] Not only are children of different racial classification required to attend their own schools, but education is organized and administered by different bodies. Despite this institutional separation, the white model of education has, since 1967, become the cornerstone for other population groups. Thus, the white history syllabus is now used in both Indian and coloured secondary schools and in a modified form in black secondary schools. In the discussion that follows the system for each group will be treated separately in order to highlight the differences where these occur.

The second point is that there is considerable inequality in the allocation of human and material resources for the education of the different population groups. This disparity is particularly acute between education for white and black children. For example, while primary and secondary education is compulsory and free for the former, this is not yet the case for black children, who despite some recent concessions in the form of free textbooks and the promise of compulsory primary education, must still frequently pay their own school fees (SAIRR. 1981. p. 465). At the same time, the per capita expenditure on white education is almost ten times that for black education, as illustrated in Table 3.

---

1. Occasional exceptions to this rule may occur in private education.

TABLE 3. Per capita expenditure on education 1978-79

Population group	Per capita expenditure (rand)[1]
White	724.00
Indian	357.15
Coloured	225.54
Black[2]	71.28

1. Includes capital expenditure.
2. Living in white areas.
Source: SAIRR, 1981, p. 460.

Black children are further disadvantaged educationally in that there are fewer teachers within the black school system, resulting in larger classes and frequently the need for double teaching sessions. This is illustrated by the high teacher–pupil ratio for blacks, indicated in Table 4. Many teachers in the black educational system have only the most basic of qualifications. For example, it can be estimated that in 1979 only 20 per cent of teachers in black schools had themselves completed a full secondary education.[1]

TABLE 4. Teacher–pupil ratios, 1980

Population group	Ratio
White	1:18.6
Coloured	1:28.8
Indian	1:25.6
Black[1]	1:45.9

1. Excludes figures from 'independent homelands'.
Source: SAIRR, 1981, p. 460.

For the reasons outlined above, only a fraction of black children who start primary school actually complete a full primary and secondary education. A gradual process of filtering out occurs, to the extent that almost half the school intake drops out before the end of the first four years of primary school and only one in every hundred completes the entire school programme (Behr, 1978, p. 182). In this context, Table 5 shows that secondary-school pupils accounted in 1976 for only 2.67 per cent of the black population as compared with 7.73 per cent of the white population.

It is the inadequate allocation of resources and consequent lower-quality education which has largely given rise to the protests and boycotts in non-white South African schools during recent years. While particular grievances may have sparked off protests at different times and in different places (such as the opposition to Afrikaans as a medium of instruction in Soweto), they have in common a demand for better-quality education and increased opportunity. Indeed, protests against education are only part of what one writer has called 'a reaction against some felt deep-seated inadequacy in the socio-political and economic system of the country' (Noruwana, 1980, p. 2).

1. Estimated from data in Department of Education and Training, 1979.

TABLE 5. Percentage of population at primary and secondary schools, 1976

Population group	Population		Pupils as percentage of population group	
	Number (millions)	Percentage of total	Primary	Secondary
Black	18.63	70.6	18.26	2.67
Coloured	2.43	9.6	23.87	4.39
Indian	0.75	2.9	18.90	7.77
White	4.32	16.9	13.54	7.73
TOTAL	26.13	100.0	18.01	3.83

Source: SAIRR, 1979, p. 11.

In response to the protests, the South African Government commissioned the Human Sciences Research Council (HSRC) in 1980 to conduct an investigation into South African education. The findings of this investigation (the De Lange Report) were tabled in the South African parliament on 8 October 1981, and recommended, among other things, the creation of a single ministry of education in place of the existing system of separate education departments for each of the four main 'races'; equality of educational opportunity for all groups and a programme to eliminate race as a criterion for admission to educational institutions. However, in a preliminary white paper issued in response to the report, the government reaffirmed its commitment to the policy of separate education departments and to racially segregated schools (Lawrence, 1981).

White education

HISTORY

Three interrelated themes dominate the history of white education in South Africa. The first concerns the role of the Church; the second involves the controversial issue of the language of instruction in schools (i.e. Afrikaans v. English); and the third relates to Afrikaner Nationalist philosophy and policy towards education.

Behr (1978) has observed that the role of the Church in education can be traced to the early Dutch settlers at the Cape, who brought with them a tradition of religious education which laid emphasis on an ability to read the Bible. As the white population migrated inland during the eighteenth and nineteenth centuries, the Dutch Reformed Church established schools where new communities settled. At a less formal level, private schools were set up on farms, which catered for children from neighbouring homesteads.

The challenge to church control over education came during British rule at the Cape in the nineteenth century. From 1820 a system of secular education was established under the aegis of the state, based on the English model of education. A typical pattern which emerged was one where local communities ran their own schools, which were in turn subsidized and inspected by education authorities, who normally prescribed the curriculum.

The anglicization of education was, however, fiercely resisted in the Transvaal where, during its period as an independent Boer republic (1852-99), a system of education developed that was heavily orientated towards religion and taught in the Dutch language. Following the second Anglo-Boer War (1899-1902), the Transvaal became a British colony and secular education was introduced, with English as the medium of instruction. In reaction to this, the Dutch Reformed Church set up its own privately run system of Christian National schools, which taught through the medium of Dutch as well as English. When the Transvaal became a self-governing colony in 1907, these schools were absorbed into the state system under the 1907 Education Act, which provided for instruction in both languages.

In 1910 the former self-governing colonies of the Cape, Natal, Orange Free State and the Transvaal became provinces within the Union of South Africa. Control of primary and secondary education was retained at the provincial level and English and Dutch (later replaced by Afrikaans) were made the official languages with equal status. For the next thirty years or so, both languages could be used as a medium of instruction within the same schools, though this tended to become the exception rather than the rule.

In 1948 the Afrikaner National Party came to power and began to implement its policies of apartheid. In education this meant even stricter enforcement of segregation of schools and a clear definition of the functions of education for the four population groups. A concrete policy statement on white education was produced in 1967 in the form of the National Education Policy Act, of which the substance is reproduced in Appendix 4. The main significance of this act was that, for the first time, the central government prescribed in specific terms the character of education in white schools throughout the country. In organizational terms, this Act provided for greater control and national co-ordination of white education, and it is the main item of legislation on which the present system is based. It has also provided, in some respects, a structural model for the other population groups.

Of particular relevance to this study is the fact that the Act states that education shall have 'Christian character', a 'broad national character', and that 'the mother tongue (English or Afrikaans) shall be the medium of instruction' (see Appendix 4).

Malherbe has suggested that the elimination of dual-medium schools represented a triumph for a narrow form of Afrikaner nationalism and the achievement of a long-sought-after goal of the proponents of Afrikaner culture. This author also suggests that by isolating Afrikaans-speaking children through compulsory mother-tongue instruction, they could more easily be indoctrinated with the political dogmas of the National Party (Malherbe, 1977, p. 145). Appendix 2, Table 1, shows that in 1978 62 per cent of white secondary pupils received their education through the medium of Afrikaans nationally, and 68 per cent in the Transvaal.

The Christian National ethic embodied in the National Education Policy Act is one which traces its early roots to the Christian National schools established in the Transvaal at the turn of the century. The idea that education should be based on 'Christian National' principles was resurrected again in the 1930s when Afrikaner nationalist sentiment was growing. At a congress held in 1939 by the Federasie van Afrikaanse Kultuurvereniginge (an extreme group linked to the Broederbond—an Afrikaner secret society), an Institute for Christian National Education was founded. This institute formulated and published a document ten years later in 1949, which outlined its policy for Christian

National Education (CNE). Among its aims for the education of white Afrikaans-speaking children were that religion should be the key subject in schools and that teaching should be 'nationalist' (Afrikaner). Of history, this document (Rose and Tunmer, 1975, p. 123) had to say in Article 6:

We believe that history must be taught in the light of the divine revelation and must be seen as the fulfilment of God's decree [*raadsplan*] for the world and humanity.... Youth can faithfully take over the task and vocation of the older generation only when it has acquired through instruction in history a true vision of the origin of the nation, and of the direction in that heritage. We believe that next to the mother tongue, that patriotic [*vaderlandse*] history of the nation is the great means of cultivating love of one's own.

To further the policy of CNE, an Interchurch Commission on Education was formed in 1953 which presented memoranda to the government on the need for a CNE policy. The publication of this programme provoked an outcry from teachers and members of the public, which was strong enough to prevent it being introduced as official policy in schools. Nevertheless, the authors of the document and proponents of CNE were highly influential and the basic tenets underlying the philosophy have remained a pervasive influence in white education.

In a study of history syllabuses and textbooks in the 1960s, Auerbach found that the essential element of the CNE philosophy was present both in the aims of the Transvaal history syllabus and in some of the textbooks examined (Auerbach, 1965, p. 117). In the present study, our examination of the aims of the history syllabus in the Transvaal also suggests that a Christian National perspective remains (see Chapter 4).

ADMINISTRATION OF WHITE EDUCATION

While overall responsibility is vested in the Minister of National Education, who directs the Department of National Education, primary and secondary education is administered by the four provincial education departments, which are responsible for the schools within their jurisdiction. No legislation can be passed at provincial level, however, without the approval of the Minister of National Education. The latter is advised on general education policy for schools by the National Education Council, which includes the directors of the four provincial education departments.

TABLE 6. Number of white primary and secondary schools in South Africa, 1979

Type of school	All provinces	Transvaal
Provincial schools	2 192	900
Provincial aided	77	10
Private	142	39
TOTAL	2 411	949

Source: South Africa, 1981.

The number of white primary and secondary schools in South Africa and in the Transvaal is shown in Table 6. Approximately 39 per cent of all South Africa's white schools are located in the Transvaal.

Primary and secondary education is free for white children in South Africa and schools are financed by the provinces from tax revenue and central government subsidies.

ENROLMENT IN WHITE SCHOOLS

It is compulsory for white children to attend school from the beginning of the year in which they reach 7 years of age until the end of the year in which they turn 16 or have passed the school-leaving examination—whichever comes first.

Figures for white enrolment are outlined in Appendix 2, Tables 1 and 2. The latter shows that in 1980 primary schools accounted for 64 per cent of total national white enrolment and secondary schools for 36 per cent. Earlier figures (1978) shown in Appendix 2, Table 1, indicate that the Transvaal accounted for 53 per cent of national white secondary-school enrolment.

ORGANIZATION OF WHITE EDUCATION

In 1962, a system of differentiated education, providing different types of curricula (e.g. commercial or technical) was introduced in white South African secondary schools. This has also been adopted for the other population groups. Under this system, a twelve-year structure of schooling is divided into four distinct phases, each consisting of three years. This system is outlined in Table 7.

TABLE 7. Structure of white education

School level	Class	Year of study	Age range
Junior primary	Substandard A	1	
	Substandard B	2	6-8
	Standard 1	3	
Senior primary	Standard 2	4	
	Standard 3	5	9-11
	Standard 4	6	
Junior secondary	Standard 5	7	
	Standard 6	8	12-14
	Standard 7	9	
Senior secondary	Standard 8	10	
	Standard 9	11	15-17
	Standard 10	12	

Since our study is concerned principally with aspects of secondary education, this section will concentrate on the final two phases of the school structure, i.e. the junior secondary and senior secondary phases. It must be pointed out that although Standard 5 is considered to be the first year of the secondary syllabus it is normally taught in the last year of primary school.

The junior secondary phase

The junior secondary phase is broadly based, and most subjects are compulsory. These are outlined in Table 8.

TABLE 8. Subjects taught during the junior secondary phase

Examination subjects	Non-examination subjects
The two official languages (Afrikaans and English) Mathematics General science History/geography[2] Basic techniques (e.g. art, handicrafts etc)	Scripture Physical education Youth preparedness[1]

1. Youth preparedness programmes are given throughout the school system and are aimed at 'strengthening pupils' moral sense'. This will be examined more thoroughly in Chapter 7.
2. History is compulsory up to Standard 7 in the Transvaal.

At Standard 5, subject learning takes over from class teaching, and at the end of this year pupils must make a provisional choice as to the field of study to be pursued in the senior secondary phase when the system of differentiated education takes effect. This choice will, in turn, determine the type of secondary or high school which he or she will attend. For example, if the pupil does not attain the requisite academic standard, a practical syllabus with a vocational bias will be pursued.

The senior secondary phase

It is at this level (Standards 8 to 10) that the pupil is offered differentiated courses or fields of study, and it is also at this level that he or she is prepared for the final school-leaving examination (matriculation). The successful completion of this examination enables the pupil to enter university or other institutions of further education.

During the senior secondary phase, the pupil pursues one of the following eight fields: agriculture, arts, commerce, general, home economics, humanities, natural science or technical. Each field of study comprises a curriculum made up of six examination subjects and some compulsory non-examination subjects (scripture, physical education and youth preparedness). Of the six examination subjects, two must be the official language, two intrinsic to the field of study, and two complementary to the field.

The candidate's choice of field of study is determined not only by his or her preference or ability, but also by regulations laid down by particular education departments, by the courses that schools are able to offer, and by the entrance requirements of universities and colleges. The Transvaal provides lists of subject groupings from which candidates must choose. These are based on particular fields of study and assigned to particular schools. Subjects may be taken at a standard or higher grade and separate syllabuses are drawn up for the two grades. For admission to university in South Africa, at least four subjects, including both official languages, must be passed at the Higher grade.

Co-ordination of syllabuses and examinations

In order to co-ordinate syllabuses, courses and examination standards on a national basis, core syllabuses are drawn up by subject committees composed of representatives of all the education departments. This core syllabus is prescribed nationally but each provincial department of education can add up to 30 per cent to the core in order to take account of local circumstances.

The co-ordination of examination standards is overseen by the Joint Matriculation Board (JMB), which is a statutory body set up to control admission to South African universities. All education departments and all universities are represented on the JMB.

The school-leaving examination (Senior Certificate or matriculation) is taken at the end of Standard 10 and is conducted by the four provincial education departments, the Department of National Education, the departments responsible for coloured and Indian education, and the JMB itself (mostly in private schools). All these departments issue their own certificates to successful candidates, which if judged to be of a high enough standard are given matriculation exemption by the JMB. By moderating the examination papers and scripts of the various education departments, the JMB thus ensures that equivalent standards are maintained throughout the country. With a matriculation or matriculation exemption certificate, the pupil is eligible to enter university. Pupils with a Senior Certificate without matriculation exemption are eligible for admission to other tertiary institutions such as technical colleges and primary teacher-training courses, as well as to diploma courses at universities. Table 9 shows the number and type of school-leaving certificates issued to white pupils in 1978. From this it will be seen that the Transvaal Education Department (TED) accounted for the greatest number of matriculation exemption certificates and for 48 per cent of certificates without exemption.

TABLE 9. School-leaving certificates awarded by white education departments, 1978

Education Department	Type of certificate		Total	Percentage of total
	Matric./matric. exemption	Other		
TED	11 075	9 956	21 031	46.7
Other provincial depts	9 704	12 174	21 878	48.5
Dept of National Education	195	470	665	1.5
JMB	1 129	380	1 509	3.3
TOTAL	22 103	22 980	45 083	100.0

Source: South Africa, 1981.

Black education

HISTORY

The first network of schools for South Africa's black population were set up by the various church missionary societies who came to South Africa during the nineteenth century. From then until the 1950s, education was controlled almost exclusively by the churches and by provincial education departments.

In the Transvaal, there were some 200 mission schools by 1903 and education as such stressed moral and religious values (Behr, 1978, p. 161). After the formation of the Union of South Africa in 1910, the provincial governments provided grants-in-aid to black schools which came from a poll tax levied on blacks specifically for this purpose. During the decades which followed, African education developed very slowly and a government committee of inquiry reported in 1935 that over 70 per cent of black children of school age were not attending school. The same committee also deplored both interdenominational rivalry in education and the conditions under which many pupils were being educated (Welsh Report, 1936).

In 1949, after the National Party came to power, a commission was set up to consider the future of education for Africans. As part of its terms of reference the commission was instructed to formulate plans for the provision of 'education for Natives as an independent race, in which their past and present inherent racial qualities, their distinct characteristics and aptitude, and their needs under ever-changing social conditions' were to be taken into consideration (Rose and Tunmer, 1975, p. 244).

The report produced by the commission, the Eiselen Report (Union of South Africa, 1951), drew a clear distinction between white and black education, and formed the basis of subsequent legislation affecting education for blacks. The main recommendations were incorporated in the Bantu Education Act of 1953, which was introduced by Dr H. F. Verwoerd, the then Minister of Native Affairs.

The Bantu Education Act transferred the control of education from the missionaries and the provinces to central government, where it was administered by the Department of Native Affairs. In 1958, a separate Department of Bantu Education was created, with its own minister (now called the Department of Education and Training). Under the provisions of this Act, emphasis was placed on the first four years of primary school, with instruction in the mother tongue.

The organization of black schools was, according to Malherbe, essential to the overall policy of apartheid which the National Party started to implement soon after it came to power in 1948. This new system of education for blacks also paved the way for the abolition of missionary influence, which the government considered to be too liberal (Malherbe, 1977, p. 545).

In a now-famous speech given before the Senate in 1954 (quoted in Rose and Tunmer, 1975, pp. 265-6), Dr Verwoerd gave a clear indication of the new educational policy for black people:

It is the policy of my department that [Bantu] education would have its roots entirely in the Native areas and in the Native environment and Native community. There Bantu education must be able to give itself complete expression, and there it will perform its real service. The Bantu must be guided to serve his own community in all respects.

There is no place for him in the European Community above the level of certain forms of labour. Within his own community, however, all doors are open. For that reason it is of no avail for him to receive a training which has as its aim absorption in the European community, where he cannot be absorbed.

One immediate result of the Bantu Education Act was a rapid increase in the number of children in school, with the school population doubling between 1955 and 1965. In the following decade, there was a 90 per cent increase in total enrolment and an almost fivefold increase of pupils in secondary schools. However, as Malherbe has pointed out, despite this increase in enrolment, the resources invested in black education did not keep pace in real terms, with the result that the average quality of the teaching suffered (Malherbe, 1977).

Another consequence of the Bantu Education Act was that the process of decentralization of the control of education to the homelands also gathered momentum, with government policy (in line with its overall philosophy of separate development and its view of the urban African as a temporary resident) being to concentrate secondary education and teacher training in the homelands.

In 1980 a new Education and Training Act (1979), which replaced the 1953 act, came into effect. This makes provision *inter alia* for the introduction of compulsory primary education and pre-school education for black children.

ADMINISTRATION OF BLACK EDUCATION

The authority responsible for black education is the Department of Education and Training in Pretoria. It has two functions: the first is to exercise direct control over all school and post-school education (excluding universities) for black children living in white areas of South Africa. Its second function is to act as a central liaison, planning and co-ordinating authority for the education departments of the 'dependent' homelands.

The administration of black education in white areas is decentralized into six regions, each with its own director and each responsible for a number of school inspection circuits. Local responsibility for school management is commonly in the hands of school committees. The structure of educational administration in the homelands follows almost exactly that of the Department of Education and Training.

Most black schools are state-aided; 1979 figures show that approximately 52 per cent were community-run and 41 per cent were farm schools. In the same year, only 3 per cent were fully financed by the state (Department of Education and Training, 1979). Community schools are subsidized by the Department of Education and Training through payment of techers' salaries, furniture and equipment, and most recently the introduction of free textbooks in some schools. In white areas, grants are given for building schools which are repaid by the imposition of housing levies on residents in townships.[1] Farm schools are built by farm-owners for the children of their employees and receive the same subsidies as community schools. With the allocation of public resources to black education insufficient to meet the growing requirements, the private sector has increasingly contributed towards black education, particularly in the homelands.

TABLE 10. Number of black schools in South Africa and the Transvaal, 1979

Area	Primary schools		Secondary schools	
	Number	%	Number	%
Black states[1]	3 942	38.6	805	76.7
White areas	6 275	61.4	245	23.3
TOTAL	10 217	100.0	1 050	100.0
Transvaal	2 106	33.5[2]	135	55.1[2]

1. Excludes independent homelands.
2. Black schools in Transvaal as a percentage of black schools in white areas.
Source: Department of Education and Training, 1980*a*, pp. 20-1.

---

1. In 1980 the Department of Education and Training undertook full responsibility for building schools so that levies previously used for this purpose can either be abolished or used for helping schools with additional equipment and facilities.

Table 10 shows the number of black primary and secondary schools in South Africa and the Transvaal. From this it will be seen that there are approximately three times as many secondary schools in the homelands as in white areas and that more than 55 per cent of black secondary schools in white areas are located in the Transvaal.

ENROLMENT IN BLACK SCHOOLS

Education for black children, unlike for the other population groups in South Africa, is neither compulsory nor universally free, although the Education and Training Act of 1979 makes provision for the gradual introduction of compulsory primary education. The 1979 figures for enrolment in black schools are given in Appendix 2, Tables 3, 4 and 5. From this it can be seen that a greater number of pupils are enrolled in primary and secondary schools in black states than in white areas; total enrolment is significantly greater in primary schools (85.3 per cent) than in secondary schools (14.7 per cent), reflecting the high drop-out rate in the black education system; and 59 per cent of enrolment in secondary schools in white areas is in the Transvaal.

ORGANIZATION OF BLACK EDUCATION

Since 1976, the structure of black education has been modified to conform more closely to the structure of other education departments in South Africa. A four-phase system is in operation but, unlike the white system, the lower primary phase extends over four years. This has been designed to meet the minimum requirements of functional literacy (Behr, 1978, p. 176). The four-phase structure in black schools is outlined in Table 11. From this it can be seen that Standards 3 to 5 comprise the higher primary phase, at the end of which a Higher Primary examination is taken. This examination must be passed before a pupil can proceed to secondary school and the Higher Primary Certificate may be required for entry into some employment. The junior secondary phase covers the eighth, ninth and tenth years of school. Standard 8 constitutes the

TABLE 11. Four-phase system of education in black schools

School level	Class	Years of study	Examination
Lower primary	Substandard A	1	
	Substandard B	2	
	Standard 1	3	
	Standard 2	4	
Higher primary	Standard 3	5	
	Standard 4	6	
	Standard 5	7	Primary certificate
Junior secondary	Standard 6 (Form 1)	8	
	Standard 7 (Form 2)	9	
	Standard 8 (Form 3)	10	Junior certificate
Senior secondary	Standard 9 (Form 4)	11	
	Standard 10 (Form 5)	12	Matriculation/senior certificate

first year of the matriculation or Senior Certificate course, but is retained as the top class of the junior secondary school, because the Junior Certificate examination is taken at this level. This certificate provides admission to some teacher-training and technical courses. The matriculation or Senior Certificate examinations are taken in Standard 10 and are required for admission to degree and diploma courses at university.

Primary education

The curriculum for primary schools is centrally prescribed by the Department of Education and Training. In the schools located in white areas the medium of instruction up to and including Standard 2 is one of the African languages. English and Afrikaans are compulsory school subjects during this phase and according to the new Education and Training Act (1979) one of the official languages (usually English) may be used as the medium of instruction from Standard 4. The homeland education departments have introduced English as the medium from an earlier stage, usually the fourth year. The primary-school curriculum in black schools is as follows: three languages (two official and one African); mathematics; environmental studies (history and geography from Standards 3 to 5); general science; health education; religious education; music; and one practical subject (e.g. agriculture, woodwork, housecraft).

Secondary education

As in primary schools, the secondary-school curriculum is centrally laid down by interdepartmental subject committees. The syllabuses followed are those approved by all the departments of education. Throughout secondary school the medium of instruction is now most often English, with Afrikaans and the appropriate vernacular taught as subjects. In addition to this, most schools offer the usual range of academic subjects, but increasing emphasis is being given to a diversification of the curriculum by the inclusion of technical and commercial subjects.

The usual range of academic subjects offered are as follows: three languages (as in primary school); mathematics; biology; physical sciences; agricultural sciences; history; geography; Bible studies; economics; Latin; German; art; music; home economics; industrial and commercial subjects.

The Junior Certificate taken at the end of Standard 8 serves as an entrance to the senior secondary phase, as well as to teacher-training courses[1] for primary education and certain trade and technical courses. On completion of secondary school, black students mostly take the National Senior Certificate examination, which is conducted by the Department of National Education and administered by the Department of Education and Training. Matriculation exemption is awarded where sufficient standards are met in the National Senior Certificate examination. The number of candidates and pass rates for the various examination in the black school system in 1978 are shown in Table 12.

---

1. It was announced in 1980 that in future only students with a Senior Certificate would be admitted to teacher training-institutions (personal communication).

TABLE 12. Number of black students taking examinations, 1978 (full-time students only)[1]

Examination	Number of candidates	Number passed	Percentage passed
Higher Primary Certificate	204 346	114 868	70.9
Junior Certificate	94 122	62 593	66.5
School-leaving[1] examination	9 804	7 468	76.2
Matriculation exemption		3 236	
National Senior Certificate		4 232	

1. Excludes Transkei and Bophutatswana.
Source: Department of Education and Training, 1979.

Coloured education

HISTORY

As with black education, the education of children from the coloured communities was for a long time in the hands of the churches. It was not until the 1920s that the provinces became involved through the provision of grants-in-aid to mission schools. The great majority of the coloured population live in the Cape Province. In the Transvaal there were 3,978 coloured pupils enrolled in twenty-seven primary schools by 1925, and for the next quarter of a century coloured education was expanded from metropolitan areas to country towns and villages. By 1962, the number of coloured schools in the Transvaal had risen to seventy-seven with an enrolment in excess of 20,000 (Behr, 1978).

In 1964, the administration and control of coloured education was centralized, with responsibility being transferred from the provinces to the Department of Coloured Affairs, where a Division of Education was established.

ADMINISTRATION OF COLOURED EDUCATION

Since 1969, responsibility for coloured education has been vested in the Administration of Coloured Affairs (ACA) which is the administrative body of the Coloured Persons' Representative Council.[1] The ACA controls all primary and secondary educational institutions, with financial responsibility resting with the Minister for Coloured Affairs. State-aided church schools are, however, the most common category of school, particularly in the rural areas. This is reflected in the figures shown in Table 13.

1. In 1980 the Coloured Persons' Representative Council was replaced by the Coloured Persons Council.

TABLE 13. Number of primary and secondary schools for coloured pupils in South Africa, 1980

Type of school	Number	%
State schools	770	38.4
State-aided schools	1 190	59.3
Private schools	12	0.6
Other	35	1.7
TOTAL	2 007	100.0

Source: SAIRR, 1981, p. 482.

The administrative structure of education for coloured pupils is similar to the Department of Education and Training for blacks. The headquarters are in Cape Town and consist of planners, administrators and subject specialists. The administration maintains a number of regional offices in all the provinces and, at the local level, most state schools have school committees which perform an advisory and support role.

ENROLMENT IN COLOURED SCHOOLS

Primary and secondary education are free for coloured children, including books and stationery. Education became compulsory in 1974 for 7 year-olds, and was gradually extended upwards in succeeding years. From January 1980, it was compulsory up to the age of 16 or Standard 8. The enrolment figures for coloured pupils in 1980 are shown in Appendix 2. Table 6. From this it will be seen that primary enrolment was quite significantly higher (81.2 per cent) than secondary enrolment, which accounted for only 18 per cent of the total.

ORGANIZATION OF COLOURED EDUCATION

The four-phase system of education designed for white children was adapted to coloured education in 1972 (see Table 7). The curricula for the primary-school phases are much the same as those in white schools, covering the usual basic skill subjects with either English or Afrikaans (more usually the latter) as the medium of instruction.

As in the primary schools, the syllabuses followed in secondary schools are basically the same as those used in the white school system. The Administration of Coloured Affairs has also followed the white education system in introducing differentiated education at secondary level. In addition to the usual range of academic subjects, a range of technical, commercial, art and vocationally oriented subjects are offered. During the senior secondary phase, subjects may be taken at the Standard or Higher grade.

Since many coloured pupils leave school at the end of Standard 8 (the final year of compulsory education) the Junior Certificate examination is incorporated in the coloured education system. For those pupils who complete the full twelve years of schooling, a Senior Certificate examination is offered. Table 14 shows the number of coloured schoolchildren who passed these examinations in 1979. From this it will be seen that a substantially greater number of pupils passed the Junior Certificate than the school-leaving examination, and that of the latter the Senior Certificate predominated over matriculation exemptions.

TABLE 14. Examination passed by coloured pupils, 1979

Examination	Number	%
Junior Certificate	18 567	73.3
Matriculation exemption	2 456	9.7
Senior Certificate	4 323	17.0
TOTAL	25 346	100.0

Source: SAIRR, 1981, p. 484.

Indian education

HISTORY

The first schools for Indians in South Africa were started in the latter half of the nineteenth century for children of plantation workers in Natal, where most of the Indian population still lives. In the Transvaal, schools specifically for Indians were established in 1913 and by 1928 there were an estimated 1,000 Indians attending government schools in that province, with many more attending schools for coloured pupils. By 1962, the number of Indian pupils attending school in the Transvaal exceeded 20,000 (Behr, 1978).

From 1966 the control of all Indian schools was transferred from the provincial education departments to the Department of Indian Affairs, where a Division of Education was established.

ADMINISTRATION OF INDIAN EDUCATION

While the Division of Education within the Department of Indian Affairs is responsible for primary and secondary education, the department itself administers the funds for Indian education provided by the state.

The number of schools for Indians in South Africa is given in Table 15. From this, it will be seen that state schools form the largest category.

TABLE 15. Number of primary and secondary schools for Indians in South Africa, 1980

Type of school	Number	%
State schools	259	65.0
State-aided	129	32.4
Private	3	0.8
Special	7	1.8
TOTAL	398	100.0

Source: SAIRR, 1981, p. 487.

ENROLMENT IN INDIAN SCHOOLS

Education for Indian pupils is compulsory from the age of 7 to 15 and is free, including textbooks and stationery. The number of pupils enrolled in Indian schools in 1980 is shown in Appendix 2, Table 7. From this it will be seen that 69 per cent of total enrolment was at the primary level and 31 per cent at secondary.

ORGANIZATION OF INDIAN EDUCATION

The four-phase system of differentiated education designed for white schoolchildren was introduced to Indian schools in 1973 (see Table 7). Courses and syllabuses are based on nationally determined core syllabuses for white children. Tuition in all phases of the school structure is taught through the medium of English, with Afrikaans taught as a compulsory second language from Standard 1.

At the primary-school level a uniform curriculum that aims to develop basic skills and knowledge is followed. At secondary school, pupils follow either an ordinary or a practical course. During the junior secondary phase pupils following the ordinary course are exposed to a broad spectrum of subjects and a choice of field is made for the final phase. At this stage, the fields of study offered are as follows: general, humanities, natural science, commerce, home economics and technical.

Most subjects in these fields are offered in the Standard and Higher grades. The subjects are, as in white education, laid down in accordance with the requirements of the JMB. Pupils take a school-leaving examination at the end of Standard 10 (Senior Certificate), which, if recognized to be of sufficiently high standard, is given matriculation exemption by the JMB. Figures for 1979 are shown in Table 16.

TABLE 16. Examinations passed by Indian pupils, 1979

Examination	Number	%
Matriculation exemption	1 595	35.1
Senior Certificate	2 954	64.9
TOTAL	4 549	100.0

Source: SAIRR, 1981, p. 488.

3 Aims and methods of textbook analysis

General trends in textbook analysis

Early work on textbook analysis can be traced to the period following the First World War when attempts were made to identify and eliminate bias in German and other European textbooks. At a more international level, analysis and revision of textbooks was promoted by the League of Nations, which, in 1925, passed the Casares Resolution recommending the exchange of textbooks between countries. The Scandinavian countries were the first to put this into practice.

The role played by the League of Nations was continued by Unesco, which, in 1949, published a guide proposing criteria for evaluating textbooks. These included accuracy, fairness, balance and worldmindedness (Unesco, 1949, pp. 78-81). Unesco also sponsored a series of international conferences on the writing and revision of textbooks for international understanding. One such conference held in Goslar, Federal Republic of Germany, recommended among other things the elimination of expressions deemed to convey hatred or contempt for other peoples or races (Unesco, 1963, p. 4).

The field of textbook analysis has been particularly concerned with historical teaching materials, which one study has cited as being the major repository of evaluative references to minorities (McDiarmid and Pratt, 1971, p. 25). Analyses of history textbooks have also revealed a high degree of nationalistic bias. One study undertaken by an Anglo-American team (Billington, 1966, p. 37) found for example that:

Nationalistic bias as it persists today is in more dangerous form than the monstrous distortions of a past generation.... It is more subtle, more persuasive, and far less easy to detect, partly because it often mirrors subconscious prejudices of which the textbook author himself is unaware. Today's textbooks plant in the minds of their readers a belief in the overall superiority of their own countries, not simply an exaggerated image of past leaders. The misconceptions, accepted unquestioningly by the students of this generation, may warp their judgements no less seriously than the mis-statements of an earlier time.

Another study conducted by Hatch on history textbooks used in the United Kingdom found that British, and to a lesser extent European, history predominated. Where attention was directed to Africa and Asia in some of these textbooks, it was the activities of European imperialists that predominated, and emphasis was put on discoverers rather than on what they discovered (Hatch, 1962, p. 64).

Research on the presentation of racial and minority groups in textbooks has mostly been carried out in North America and particularly the United States. One major study conducted by the American Council on Education in the 1940s found that immigrant minorities received unfavourable treatment and that stereotypes were frequent, particularly in the case of black people (American Council on Education, 1949, p. 31). The Civil Rights Movement in the United States during the 1960s gave impetus to further analysis of black groups in textbooks. American Indian groups also came under scrutiny at this time and research revealed that, despite the existence of much source material on Indian culture, little of this was incorporated into textbooks (Costo, 1970, p. 9). Another study found that American Indian history was generally ignored and distorted, with gold miners who seized Indian lands presented as heroes, while the Indians who opposed them were described as savages (Henry, n.d., pp. 21-4).

Another dimension of bias identified in textbook studies has been a failure on the part of authors to confront controversial issues squarely. For example, a study carried out in Michigan found that there was little or no discussion of the Ku-Klux-Klan or the Civil Rights Movement in textbooks (Michigan Committee Reports, 1968). Similarly, a study of interpretations of South Africa in British primary textbooks revealed that most books gave no account of slavery and failed to discuss apartheid (Nash, 1972).

In summarizing the findings of textbook analysis, McDiarmid and Pratt (1971, p. 25) have identified general biases of omission and commission in the treatment of minority groups. The main biases of omission are: failure to note positive contributions and qualities; failure to note the contemporary condition; and failure to note the persecution of, or discrimination against, minorities. The biases of commission are: an excessively political approach resulting in emphasis on war and conflict; unscholarly reproduction of stereotypes; and the casual use of emotive or pejorative terms to describe groups.

In their own study of textbooks used in Ontario, McDiarmid and Pratt, in addition to analysing biases in the treatment of minority groups, extended their research to examine interpretations of the labour movement, which they found tended to emphasize violence. These authors also looked at interpretations of communism in textbooks and found that evaluative terms such as 'threat' and 'menace' were used, which they concluded were likely to commit the pupils to a point of view before any facts on communism were presented (McDiarmid and Pratt, 1971, p. 95).

Analyses of South African textbooks

A fairly comprehensive study of history textbooks used in the Transvaal was carried out by Auerbach in the 1960s. The findings of this report showed that historical research carried out during the forty years prior to the analysis had not been incorporated into textbooks. Moreover, the author concluded that the education system in South Africa was being used to divide the people. This finding was based on an analysis which showed that differences existed between Afrikaans and English-language history textbooks. These differences were observed both in the importance attached to various sections of the syllabus by authors, and in their interpretations of events.

The research also showed that there was a pronounced trend to greater ethnocentrism in Afrikaans textbooks, which had influenced the content of the syllabus prescribed for all schools, irrespective of the language medium. This trend, the author noted, had been influenced by the philosophy of Christian National Education (discussed in Chapter 2). In particular, Auerbach (1965, p. 126) found that much emphasis was put on the history of Europeans in South Africa, especially Afrikaners. This history was presented as a contrast to that of other South African population groups, particularly Africans. The author concluded that as a result of these interpretations:

White children who learn history and related subjects with this emphasis are likely to obtain an exaggerated idea of the relative importance of the history of South Africa within the history of civilization, and more especially are likely to be imbued with the erroneous belief that Africans are permanently tribal and inherently inferior to Whites, and that Western Civilization and Christianity are racially linked with people of White or Caucasian stock. This will have the effect of further dividing the people

Since the Auerbach study there has been much public debate concerning the content of history textbooks, which has been reported in the South African press. Two authors, Van Jaarsveld and Joubert, have particularly come under attack. For example, Taylor noted that Van Jaarsveld, in his book *New Illustrated History, Standard 8* (for the pre-1973 syllabus), adopted a line of straight propaganda by directly praising Nationalist Party policy (Taylor, 1971). Writing four years later of the same author's new text, Lewsen (1975) pointed out that despite a change in syllabus this textbook re-used sections of the old one without any revision and that it ignored thirty years' historical evidence which showed that blacks were settled west of the Fish River before it was made a boundary. The Lewsen critique also observed that this textbook was without context, ideologically slanted and riddled with stereotypes.

Similar criticisms have also been directed towards Joubert. For example, a report in the *Star* newspaper in 1975 noted that objections had been raised against Joubert's text *History for Standard 10*, which had been (and still is) approved by the Transvaal Education Department for use in that province. The report noted that one complainant found: 'The author's approach to certain aspects of history and to some controversial policies is so unobjective as to make him a propagandist rather than a historian' (*The Star*, 1975, p. 27).

Methodological approaches to textbook analysis

In their review of textbooks analysis, McDiarmid and Pratt have observed that early research tended to concentrate on major omissions, obvious distortions and blatant expression of prejudice. During the 1920s, the conceptual basis and research design of studies on bias began to show greater rigour. New approaches involved the assessment of a more casual use of pejorative terms, the examination of stereotypes, and the employment of sampling techniques, such as selecting specific areas for analysis rather than attempting exhaustive studies of the entire history of a group. Quantitative analysis was also used to calculate the proportion of space in textbooks devoted to different countries or groups (McDiarmid and Pratt, 1971, p. 13).

In general, most research on textbooks has been of a qualitative nature. Frameworks for analysis have been primarily normative, theoretically loose and frequently defined by the nature of the study undertaken. A common tendency appears to have been for researchers to establish a set of guiding hypotheses around which their analyses are based. For example, in a recent study of ethnocentrism in Western textbooks, Preiswerk and Perrot (1978) identified a number of categories which structured their analysis. These included: the ambiguity of concepts such as culture, civilizations and race; the legitimation of European action; the transfer of European values to non-European societies; and the failure to incorporate non-European interpretations of history.

While textbook analysis has been largely based on qualitative analysis, some research (particularly in North America) has concentrated on refining quantitative techniques as an aid to evaluating texts. These techniques have included: frequency analysis, which counts the number of references given to a particular item; non-frequency analysis, which is concerned only with the presence or absence of particular references; contingency analysis, in which the frequency with which concepts are related or juxtaposed in the text are counted; and evaluative assertion analysis, which measures evaluative aspects of descriptions of specific objects or persons in the narrative along a favourable–unfavourable dimension (McDiarmid and Pratt, 1971, p. 122; Pool, 1959).

These quantitative techniques have been adopted in an attempt to give greater scientific rigour to textbook analysis by assigning words or forms of speech with numerical values and calculating scores from which a final interpretation is deduced. In adopting such approaches, researchers have sought to reduce the incidence of subjectivity in their analyses and to facilitate greater comparability between texts.

The process of reducing concepts to numerical indices, apart from being a very cumbersome procedure, also carries the danger of losing sight of the continuity of narrative by focusing on isolated phenomena. For example, evaluative assertion analysis tends to oversimplify the meaning of a text by reducing its content to a single positive–negative dimension when the overall picture may be considerably more complex. Similarly, while frequency analysis indicates the number of times a reference occurs in the text, this is not necessarily significant in itself since it is the 'intensity of meaning' which is likely to make the greatest impact on the reader.

Qualitative analysis, by contrast, is able to describe in greater depth how an author interprets his or her subject and to link this to more general theoretical considerations. While qualitative analysis may not be value-free, as critics have been quick to point out, neither is the risk of subjectivity entirely eradicated in quantitative analysis, since the researcher identifies the concepts for measurement and sets the rules for their classification according to his own purposes and theoretical preferences. A strictly quantitative approach is more 'scientific' than a qualitative approach only in the limited sense of offering greater replicability, but this tends to be bought at the expense of a degree of crudeness that fails to capture subtleties of meaning that may be the most relevant characteristic of the text. Where the analysis of content is concerned we have to conclude that not everything that counts can be counted, and not everything that can be counted counts.

Methodology for an analysis of South African textbooks

It is evident from a review of textbook analysis that population groups and events have frequently been examined with scant reference to the broader socio-econoz ic or political context, and that the analysis of ideology has played a minor role in the discussion of bias. Nieves Falcon (1980, p. 5) has argued that it is economic domination and ideology that underpin racist distortions in educational materials:

Books, particularly children's books and school textbooks, are one component of the media and are thus a tool for consciously promoting values which perpetuate subordination. They are one instrument which supports the existing structure of relationships between the dominating power and those dominated, i.e. between colonizer and colonized.

While analyses of textbooks may usefully elucidate forms of bias such as stereotyping or the undervaluation or disparagement of certain groups, there is a need to extend these findings to include an analysis of the ideological basis of the accounts offered. The role of ideology in the case of South Africa is particularly important since the differential treatment of different groups in enshrined in law.

Our approach in this study is one which therefore focuses on the key concept of legitimation. This may be loosely defined as the process by which, to a greater or lesser degree, consent is secured among members of a society to the existing social and political arrangements. In the context of South Africa, we have attempted to identify themes in the textbooks that tend to legitimate the philosophy and policies of apartheid.[1]

Using the notion of legitimation, we have sought to understand the ways in which authors have selected structures and omitted material in presenting their various accounts of history. In so doing, we have been particularly concerned to identify the ways in which groups of people are presented in the texts, for example through the use of stereotypes.

The concept of stereotype, indicating the tendency to attribute a fixed set of characteristics in an oversimplified and overgeneralized way to members of a group, has its usefulness, provided it is not restricted to its narrow psychological sense. One thing that became apparent in our preliminary reading of South African textbooks was that crude stereotyping of ethnic groups is not the most noticeable feature of secondary history textbook writing in South Africa. With the exception of one or two very conservative writers, explicit racial stereotypes are barely evident. The textbooks are generally quite sophisticated in style and tend towards a more fact-based rather than an opinion-oriented interpretation of history. The few textbooks that deviate from this pattern are noted in the analysis.

While explicit stereotyping is not a dominant feature of senior-level history textbooks, an implicit form of stereotyping is evident from the narratives. It is implicit in the sense that allusions are made towards certain characteristics or forms of behaviour, rather than direct ascription of values to groups. In this more oblique form, stereotyping can be inferred through the context in which

---

1. For further details on the nature of apartheid and the role of history in its legitimation, the reader is referred to the opening chapter of this book.

groups or individuals are presented, rather than identified through the use of descriptive forms.

In examining the context in which groups are presented, we have sought to identify the range and character of the motives attributed to them, as well as the depth to which these motives are explored. The evaluation of certain groups may occur not only through pejorative labelling, but also through a failure to present their case adequately.

A number of general hypotheses derived from the findings of a large body of work in the field of mass communications have been used as a framework for this study. These are as follows:

The values endorsed in school texts and popular media in any country will tend to support the existing political system of that country.

Groups that are socially and politically dominant will be more favourably presented than subordinate groups or non-dominant ethnic minorities.

Where different texts are prepared for subordinate groups, any subordinate group will be more favourably represented in its 'own' textbooks than in those prepared for other groups, particularly the dominant one.

The images of foreign countries promoted by the texts in any country will be influenced by that country's historical relations with those countries and by its present foreign policy.

Structure of the analysis

The first part of the analysis (Chapter 4) comprises a quantitative analysis of a large sample of textbooks used in South African secondary schools. We have used the history syllabus as a framework for the analysis and have measured the proportion of space allocated by authors to topics specified by the syllabus. Calculations are made on the basis of page counts which are then converted to percentage form. We have used this quantitative approach to assess the weighting given to different categories of subject-matter.

The value of the quantitative analysis in Chapter 4 is that it has allowed us to survey the entire secondary history syllabus and to obtain a composite picture of a large sample of textbooks. However, a quantitative analysis based on subject groupings has its limitations because it reveals nothing of what is actually being said. This is the role of the qualitative analysis given in Chapters 5, 6 and 7. Nevertheless, a quantitative analysis of the type we have adopted has allowed us to identify themes which have been emphasized to the exclusion of others. This, in turn indicates the priorities and values of authors who, although constrained by the syllabus, do appear to have some leeway in interpreting it.

The quantitative analysis is followed in Chapter 5 by a study of contact between white and black groups in the early nineteenth century. This period was chosen because it represents a watershed in South African history. Conflict between black and white groups and between the Boers and the British authorities combined to generate a sense of grievance and common interest among many of the Dutch-speaking colonists of the Eastern Cape. Many writers trace the origins of Afrikaner nationalism back to this time and the events of the period remain an important part of its mythology. The way that history textbooks deal with this period may therefore be taken as a critical case in assessing their ideological significance.

Chapter 6 is intended to complement the preceding analysis by examining interpretations of contemporary South African history (1919 70). We have selected this period for two reasons. Firstly, its inclusion in the final-year syllabus (Standard 10) shows that it is thought to be important by those responsible for educational policy. Secondly, since South African policies of racial discrimination and segregation have been extended and formalized during this period, any ideological biases in the texts seem most likely to show up in the extent to which textbook authors deal with or avoid these issues and the philosophy of apartheid as it has developed. The events of recent years have intensified the divisions within South African society and it is therefore illuminating to examine how different authors have treated the contentious issues that have implications for the lives of children from all sections of the community.

The final portion of the analysis, Chapter 7, is concerned with interpretations of the contemporary history of the rest of Africa. The topic has been selected for study because it concerns decolonization and the establishment of black majority rule on the African continent. These events have direct implications for South Africa both in terms of her relations with neighbouring states as well as her own subjugated black population. Indeed it is by no means accidental that apartheid, with its emphasis on separate tribal 'homelands', was introduced at a time when independence movements were gathering momentum elsewhere on the African continent. It is interesting therefore to see how textbook authors treat change in Africa and whether they draw any parallels with South Africa.

Both Chapters 6 and 7 of the analysis are concerned with history textbooks written for Standard 10, which is the final year of secondary school in South Africa. Apart from what has been said above, there are two particular reasons for examining this level of the education system. Firstly, the Standard 10 syllabus forms the basis for national school leaving examinations, which are moderated by a common body, the Joint Matriculation Board (for further details, see Chapter 2). As a result of this national co-ordination, the Standard 10 syllabus shows considerable conformity throughout South Africa's various education systems, whether defined by province or ethnic grouping. Thus, all children who study history in their final year of secondary school will be exposed to the same content. This would not necessarily be the case at more junior levels, particularly in black education, and by focusing on Standard 10 we are thereby assured of a more representative national sample.

The second reason for selecting Standard 10 textbooks is that, being the most senior study materials, they should represent the most sophisticated approach to the subject and be able to give some appreciation of historical methods. It should be expected therefore that these textbooks transcend the level of mere facts or opinions and provide reasoned arguments in support of the material presented, thereby providing students with the opportunity of drawing their own conclusions. It would be expected, for example, that the possibility of explicit stereotypes or overt ideological perspectives be minimized. If, on the other hand, such obvious forms of bias are present at this level, then it can be assumed that the incidence of bias is likely to be even greater in more junior textbooks.

The textbook sample

The textbook sample used in this study is based on the list of English-language history texts approved by the Transvaal Education Department for use in white schools in the Transvaal, and a selection of textbooks written for the black education system. The one exception to this occurs in Chapter 4, the quantitative analysis, where the sample has been increased to include a selection of textbooks used in other provinces.

Our reasons for selecting the Transvaal are twofold. Firstly, the Transvaal is the most populous of the four provinces and contains more than 50 per cent of both South Africa's white school population and its black school population in white areas. Since the syllabus used in white education is also prescribed in Indian, coloured and, at the senior level, in black education it is likely that these texts will also be used by non-white groups. The textbooks approved for the Transvaal therefore appear as the most appropriate choice in a study of this kind—in which it was not feasible to examine all textbooks in use in South Africa—because more children are exposed to these than to books written for any other province. In any case, books for different provinces do not vary greatly since all have to conform to the core syllabus.

The second reason for using Transvaal approved texts is that these are provided free in state schools, which means that the vast majority of white children in the Transvaal use them. The procedures by which textbooks are selected by the Transvaal Education Department are more fully described in Chapter 4. There is a limited number of books on the approved list. For example, in Standard 10 only two books in English are recommended. This has important implications in that it severely limits the choice available to pupils and maintains a high degree of standardization in what is taught.

Our sample also includes a small number of textbooks written for the black education system in South Africa. These have been selected to determine whether these books provide different perspectives from those for white pupils. In particular, we have been interested to see whether the texts for black pupils give greater emphasis to the history of South Africa's black population.

For the sake of consistency we have based our analysis on books in the English language. Most of these are also available in Afrikaans; many are translations of the Afrikaans originals. Occasionally, we have made reference to the Afrikaans versions where this has seemed useful, or where we were not able to obtain an English version.

While all the textbooks included in our sample are written to conform to a common syllabus, it is noticeable that authors have adopted distinct approaches to the material and that a variety of styles and methods is evident. It will be illuminating therefore to determine how far a consensus of opinion is present despite apparent differences in approach.

It should be stressed here that it is not our intention in this study to attribute blame or intent to particular authors, but rather to try to show that history is a vehicle for conveying themes and concepts that reflect different sociological and psychological views of the world.

Mention should also be made here of some of the constraints that are likely to be imposed on South African textbook writers. The writing of history for school texts is likely to be circumscribed by a number of factors in any country, for example by the syllabus and demands of the publisher. Beyond this, however, even greater social constraints are likely to be imposed by the nature of the education system itself and by prevailing norms and values.

In a country that is as politically divided and authoritarian in structure as South Africa, the writing of textbooks is likely to be subject to even greater constraints. In writing on a topic such as apartheid, for example, the author who wishes to have his or her book adopted by an education department is unlikely to present a critical interpretation of government policies.

4 The distribution of subject-matter

Introduction

This chapter is devoted to a quantitative analysis of history textbooks written for use in South African secondary schools. The sample is composed of forty-two textbooks, of which seventeen are approved for use in the Transvaal and twenty-one are used in other provinces. The remaining four textbooks are written for the black education system. We have used the history syllabus as a framework for the analysis, and measured the proportion of space allocated by authors to the different topics specified in the syllabus. These results are detailed in the tables in Appendix 3, which are also intended to serve as a reference for the reader, since they list the subject-matter laid down in the syllabus, standard by standard.

The syllabus

There is a high degree of uniformity in the secondary history syllabuses used by all the population groups in South Africa. Co-ordination is provided by a core syllabus, drawn up by a special committee (composed of representatives of all the education departments) and prescribed for national use. This core must constitute 70 per cent of the curriculum used in the four provinces for white education, and is also adopted by the departments responsible for coloured and Indian education, and by the Department of Education and Training for the last three years of black secondary education. These departments may in turn add up to 30 per cent to the core syllabus in order to take account of local circumstances, but they may not subtract from it.

The syllabus examined in this analysis was introduced in 1973 and is still in use today. It is divided into two sections: a junior secondary phase (Standards 5, 6 and 7) and a senior secondary phase (Standards 8, 9 and 10). Each phase is, in turn, divided into a general history and a South African history section. Standard 5 of the junior phase is taught in the final year of primary school, and covers an earlier period of history, which is outlined in Appendix 3, Tables 2 and 3. Since the analysis is concerned with history as taught at secondary school, we shall concentrate on Standards 6 and 7 of the junior phase. The senior secondary phase of the syllabus deals mainly with aspects of nineteenth- and twentieth-century history, much of which is also covered in Standards 6 and 7 of the junior secondary phase. The content of the Standard 6 and 7 textbooks in our sample is structured in two different ways. Some of the books (including those approved for Transvaal Education Department schools) are organized broadly under the main syllabus headings. Others, though they cover the same ground, are organized around important historical personalities. Since it is difficult to reduce one type of structure to the other for purposes of space comparison, data for the two kinds of structure has been presented in separate tables.

Aims of the history syllabus

The Transvaal Education Department includes, for the guidance of teachers, a list of 'aims' as an integral part of its history syllabus. The aims for the senior secondary syllabus are reproduced in Appendix 5. A perusal of these aims gives some insight into the kind of thinking that would appear to underlie educational policy. The list is wide-ranging and miscellaneous and extends well beyond an understanding of history itself. For example, Aim 3.19: 'To improve in the appreciation of literature, art, sculpture, architecture and music'. Some aims are very general for instance, '3.14. The development of the imagination and the ability to think in the abstract.' Some are psychologically oriented—for example, '3.3. To help the child in the development of an own [sic] personality'—while others are obscure: '3.21. The philosophical concept of history must be brought home to the child'.

One of the aims is '3.5. The fostering of firm principles and religious convictions'. This may perhaps be an echo of the ideal of Christian National Education discussed in Chapter 2. There is also a heavy emphasis on nationalism. Part of Aim 3.12 reads:

Development of the idea of nationality: the fostering of loyalty, respect and love for the country and its people; love and respect for one's ancestors; the elimination of prejudices.
Cultural development: the building up of an understanding of our own traditions, the fostering of respect for our own cultural and spiritual values and for those of other groups.

The latter part of this quotation alludes to the notion of 'cultural identity' which in part underlies the philosophy of separate development.

A degree of authoritarianism, a certain puritanism, and an admiration for heroic qualities are suggested in the way the aims are presented. Some idea of the flavour of this introductory section of the syllabus may be gleaned from the following aims.

3.6 To help the pupil to realize that matters that are of value to his time, such as freedom of worship, political development and independence, were won by previous generations through struggle and sacrifice.
3.10 To obtain an insight into the nature of man and into those things that are eternally part of man, such as strife, intolerance, leadership and discipleship.
3.12 ... each child must realize that he is a member of a community, a cultural group, a nation, a party, a church, a state, with duties and privileges.

At least two of the more obviously academic aims offer some basis for the evaluation of textbooks written to conform to the syllabus.

3.9. To educate to an objective approach towards history, fostering the habit of first investigating all relevant facts before passing judgement.
3.17. The child should learn to reason and to think independently.

Textbooks

In general the history textbooks in our sample have all been written to conform closely with the syllabus. Most of the authors are or have been teachers or school inspectors or otherwise involved in the educational system. The process for selecting textbooks varies among education departments. Since this study is primarily concerned with texts used in the Transvaal, the discussion will focus on the procedure adopted in that province.

In the Transvaal special committees are appointed by the Education Department to approve texts which will then be used in white provincial schools. Publishers submit textbooks to these committees for consideration. In the case of history texts, it would appear that these texts are not always in printed form and that some publishers present manuscripts for scrutiny, which can then be returned for modification as a condition of approval. Thus the degree of control exercised over content may extend beyond that imposed by the syllabus.

The Transvaal Education Department issues a list of approved textbooks from which schools decide which books to use. The choice of texts in the Transvaal is quite limited, offering an average of two to three texts per standard per language group, although books approved may change from time to time. Nevertheless, once a school has made the decision to invest in a particular book, it may, as in other countries, have to serve as the prescribed text for a few years. Thus the appearance of a revised edition or new text may not mean the immediate disappearance of an earlier edition or the adoption of a new book. Most of the Transvaal texts are available in both Afrikaans and English.

In the black education system there is a heavy dependency on the textbook as the sole form of learning material because of the paucity of funds available. Moreover, black student teachers themselves may have to learn their history from school textbooks, since some training colleges have little else in the way of source materials.

Analysis of general *v.* South African history

The history syllabus is divided between general history and South African history. The question of what proportion of text should, ideally, be devoted to each section is a debatable one. Auerbach (1965, p. 23) has argued that a ratio of 60:40 in favour of general history may be considered desirable in the South African context. The balance between the two is one indication of the breadth of approach to the subject, and the ratio is therefore looked at from this point of view.

Appendix 3, Table 1 shows the proportion of space allocated by different textbooks to general and South African history for Standards 6 to 10. These are based on page counts of text, including maps and illustrations but excluding

TABLE 17. Percentage of space allocated to general and South African history

Standard	General history	South African history	
6	48	52	} Junior secondary
7	57	43	
8	37	63	
9	49	51	} Senior secondary
10	53	47	

exercises. The general trend of the figures may be summarized by taking rounded median values of each column of the table, as shown in Table 17.

This illustrates how in most texts there is increasing emphasis on general history at the expense of South African history as the senior secondary course progresses, the greatest attention to general history being given in Standard 10. Standard 7, the last year of the junior secondary syllabus, also has a high proportion of space devoted to general history. The Standard 10 general history syllabus is entirely concerned with twentieth-century history, and the Standard 7 syllabus predominantly so. Thus it would seem that contemporary world history is seen as important by those who draw up the syllabus, rather than earlier periods of general history. The standards in which more space tends to be given to South African history (Standards 6, 8 and 9), on the other hand, deal with events, particularly the Great Trek and the Anglo-Boer wars, that are generally seen to have been crucial in establishing the present shape of South African society.

Taking the sample of textbooks together, the balance between general and South African history does not depart greatly from a 50:50 ratio over the secondary curriculum as a whole. This finding is similar to that of an earlier study of South African history textbooks (Auerbach, 1965, p. 24).

General history topics

World history in the secondary history syllabus shows a tendency to be Eurocentric and focuses heavily on aspects of nationalism. It stresses moreover political history at the expense of social or intellectual history and reflects a preoccupation with conflict (e.g. wars and revolutions).

The emphasis on Europe occurs up until the twentieth century, at which point the perspective broadens to include other regions of the world. Where reference is made to the history of countries outside Europe before the twentieth century, this is mostly in relation to European colonial activities. As mentioned in the previous chapter, Hatch (1962) found a similar pattern of emphasis in British textbooks. For example, in the present case, Africa north of the Limpopo only receives attention in Standard 7 (about 10 per cent of general history under 'The Scramble for Africa', Appendix 3, Table 8), and in the Standard 9 topic 'The Partition of Africa' (between 14 and 28 per cent of the general history syllabus, Appendix 3, Table 14). Pre-colonial Africa is not dealt with at all. Similarly, Asia and Latin America are only mentioned briefly under the heading of 'Colonization up to 1800' in Standard 6 (Appendix 3, Table 4).

North America also only receives attention in Standard 6 (around 15 per cent of general history, Appendix 3, Tables 4 and 5). While reference is made to the so-called 'ancient civilizations' in Standard 5, this is only in terms of their contribution to European civilization (Appendix 3, Table 2).

The general history is not only Eurocentric but puts heavy emphasis on politics and war. Nationalism is the overriding theme. In Standard 8, for instance, the general history section deals with 'Liberalism and Nationalism in Europe to 1848', with between 24 and 38 per cent (median 29 per cent) of general history devoted to Napoleon as a national figure (Appendix 3, Table 12). Standard 9 is similar (see Appendix 3, Table 14), dealing with the period 1848 to 1918 under the headings, 'Nationalism and Democracy in Europe', 'The Partition of Africa', and 'Events Leading to World War I'. The section on 'Nationalism and Democracy in Europe', covering the Industrial Revolution and its consequences in Great Britain, and the unification of Italy and Germany, takes up between 44 and 59 per cent (median 50 per cent) of general history in the texts we examined, with the lion's share going to the latter two topics. The consequences of the Industrial Revolution are themselves dealt with in political, as well as social and economic, terms. Political history thus heavily outweighs social, intellectual or economic history.

Twentieth-century history is covered in Standard 7 (Appendix 3, Tables 8 and 9) and in Standard 10 (Table 16). The Eurocentric perspective of the eighteenth- and nineteenth-century history is broadened to take in a wider geographical area, which includes Asia, the Middle East and Africa. However, the emphasis tends to remain on Europe, and to some extent Africa, rather than the rest of the world. In Standard 7, for example, the United Nations and the birth of Israel and China in general take up less than a third of the general history space in the books, the rest being devoted mainly to Europe. In Standard 10 the topic 'International Relations' (Appendix 3, Table 16), dealing mainly with events outside Africa, including the Cold War in Europe, occupies between 24 and 31 per cent of general history in the books (median 27 per cent). The topic 'New Africa North of the Zambesi', in the same table, shows a range of emphasis from 13 to 30 per cent, with a median value of 18 per cent. The rest of the material has a strong European emphasis. Somewhat surprisingly, textbook J (see Appendix 3), which is written for the black education system, gives only 17 per cent to the topic of Africa.

Finally, Appendix 3, Table 16 indicates a heavy weighting towards 'communism' in contemporary history in Standard 10. The topics in question are: 'Communist Russia', 'The Cold War in Europe', 'Clash of Ideologies in the Far East', and 'China's Interest in Africa'. Taken together, these topics amount to between 22 and 30 per cent of the general history syllabus. This emphasis reflects an underlying preoccupation with communist influence in South Africa, which is examined in more detail in Chapter 7.

South African history topics

The dominant feature of the figures for topics of South African history is the comparatively large proportion of space given to the history of white groups at the expense of non-white groups. A secondary feature is the tendency to give heavy weighting to events in Afrikaner history, such as the Great Trek, the Boer republics and the Anglo-Boer wars, and to define history almost exclusively in terms of politics, particularly in the twentieth century.

The white-centred approach to history is evident both in the definition of syllabus topics and the weighting given to them by the textbooks. Tables 13, 15 and 17 of Appendix 3 show that the ratio of white to non-white history is particularly high in the senior secondary phase of the syllabus.

The percentage of space given to sections of the syllabus explicitly labelled as concerning non-whites is summarized in Table 18.

TABLE 18. Percentage of syllabus explicitly concerning non-whites

Standard	Syllabus headings	Percentage Range	Median
8	British policy, towards Hottentots, slaves and Bantu: southward expansion of southern Bantu	27–49	37
9	Relations between whites, Bantu and Indians	13–24	17
10	Development of non-white peoples	19–30	20

The topic of 'Southward Expansion of the Southern Bantu' that helps to swell the Standard 8 figure is a central concern in the debate over which group (white or black) arrived first in South Africa. The argument that has been put forward by apologists for apartheid is that whites settled in an 'empty land' and were then challenged by black migrants moving south. This is used to justify the current designation of most of South Africa as a white area and only small enclaves of the land as black areas.

Non-white history in Standard 8 is given greater weighting in the textbooks written for black education. Thus textbook J shows a value of 39 per cent and K a value of 49 per cent. However, this tendency is reversed in textbook J in Standards 9 and 10, for which this text gives the lowest proportion of space to non-white history, 15 and 19 per cent respectively.

In Standard 7 South African history is entirely political, dealing with twentieth-century political figures and with civics. Political history is also heavily emphasized in Standard 10 (Appendix 3, Table 17), where the topics 'Political Development' and 'Constitutional Development' together account for between 30 and 45 per cent of the texts (median 38 per cent).

Summary

The need to conform to a common core syllabus ensures that the history textbooks cover very much the same ground for each secondary-school standard, though there are variations in the emphasis given to different topics in different texts. This applies equally to textbooks prepared for use in white schools in the four provinces, in coloured and Indian education, and in the final three years of the black education system, in which broadly the same course is followed.

Over the secondary curriculum as a whole, roughly equal attention is paid to general history as to South African history. There is increased emphasis on general history and on contemporary history in the final school year.

The general history covered by the textbooks is largely Eurocentric, and comparatively little attention is paid to the history of Asia or Latin America in any part of the curriculum. Nationalism is a dominant theme in world history, and political history is stressed rather than social, economic or intellectual history. Pre-colonial Africa is virtually ignored, but attention is given to contemporary Black Africa in the final school year. Communism is a prominent theme in the contemporary history covered.

The South African history in the textbooks is predominantly a history of the white groups in South Africa; very little is offered on the history of South African blacks before the arrival of the whites. The textbooks written for black schools are similar to those prepared for whites in most respects, but tend to give more attention to black South African history at the beginning of the senior secondary course.

5 Black and white in the early nineteenth century

Introduction

In the previous chapter we examined the amount of space that the textbooks devote to the different topics specified by the secondary-school history syllabus. In this and the following two chapters we look at the treatment of some of these topics in more detail. Contact between the white and non-white groups is a central theme in South African history. In this chapter we examine the way this contact is presented with particular reference to the situation in the Eastern Cape in the first half of the nineteenth century. This is dealt with in most detail in the textbooks for Standards 6 and 8 of the white syllabus. We pay most attention to the Standard 8 textbooks since the relevant sections are often expanded versions of the Standard 6 books. In some cases whole paragraphs from Standard 6 are reproduced word for word in Standard 8. We concentrate on the three Transvaal textbooks by Joubert (1977), Van Jaarsveld (1974) and Boyce (1973c), but refer also to other texts, particularly that prepared for black pupils by Van Rensburg, Schoeman and Vorster (1976), when this seems useful. References to any of the above-mentioned authors in this chapter are to their Standard 8 textbooks, unless otherwise stated.

    The first part of the nineteenth century was chosen because it is often taken to represent a watershed in South African history. On the one hand it saw the first substantial contact and conflict between the whites and the Bantu-speaking peoples. On the other, it was the beginning of strained relations between the Dutch-speaking farmers on the Eastern Cape frontier and the British authorities. These two sets of circumstances led in part to the Great Trek and the establishment of the independent Boer republics in the interior. Afrikaner nationalism, which has been such a potent force in South Africa, is regarded by many as having had its origins in these circumstances, and the events of this period form an important part of its mythology in which the twin themes of conflict with the blacks and resisting British imperialism are prominent. The way that the history books deal with this period may therefore be taken as a critical case in assessing their ideological significance. In this chapter we take the Eastern Cape as a starting point and go on to illustrate characteristic ways in which elements of the prevailing ideology show themselves in the texts' treatment of South African history. The main developments in the Cape in the early nineteenth century were as follows.

In 1806 Great Britain seized the Cape from the Dutch for the second time. This helped to secure the sea route to India during the war with the French in which the Dutch were France's allies. In 1814 the Cape was formally transferred to British rule under an agreement with the Dutch. A succession of governors set about establishing a British form of colonial administration and anglicizing the colony. Partly as a result of pressure from the British philanthropic and anti-slavery movements, and missionaries working in the colony, various regulations were introduced at the Cape regarding the employment of non-whites and giving them legal rights. There was also a series of new regulations governing the treatment of slaves, culminating in their emancipation in 1834. The period was marked by an intensification of conflict between white and Xhosa stock-farmers on the eastern frontier in the vicinity of the Fish River. As the whites expanded eastwards, so the Xhosa were moving south and westward, pressed from behind by other Bantu-speaking tribes. This led to a series of skirmishes and frontier wars, with different governors adopting different policies. Somerset (Governor from 1814 to 1826) brought 4,000 British settlers to the Eastern Cape, partly as an anglicization measure and partly to strengthen the white presence on the frontier. Resentment of British rule by the Dutch-speaking stock-farmers and the insecurity of life on the frontier were among several factors which led about 10,000 of these farmers to leave the colony and seek new homes for themselves in the interior. This concerted movement of population is known as the Great Trek. British governors during the period were Caledon, Cradock, Somerset, Bourke, Cole, D'Urban and Grey.

Whose history?

The first and most general point to be made about the South African history presented in the books we examined is that in all of them it is a history of the whites in South Africa. The non-whites, particularly the blacks, are presented primarily as obstacles to the achievement of white objectives, as a problem to the whites. The legitimacy of white objectives, which tend to be discussed in detail, is by and large taken for granted, while the objectives of the non-whites are seldom adequately explored and their lack of legitimacy is taken as self-evident. In this respect these textbooks conform to the paradigm that has dominated and still largely dominates South African historical writing. This paradigm contains the implicit assumptions that history begins with the arrival of the whites and is primarily concerned with charting the fortunes of different white groups in establishing themselves politically, economically and socially in the southern part of Africa. In consequence, until comparatively recently, there has been little serious attempt by historians to explore the history of non-white groups. This neglect of the majority of South Africa's population is reflected in the school textbooks.

At a cursory level this white-centred perspective is evident in frequent reference to non-whites as a 'problem' (to the whites). In his Standard 6 text, for instance, Paynter (n.d.) has the subheading: 'Grey Looks for a New Approach to the Bantu Problem' (p. 157). Joubert and Jooste (1977) have '*Waaraan Grey die swartprobleem toegeskryf het*' (What Grey Attributed the Black Problem to) (p. 135). In books for Standard 8 Joubert refers to 'the Bantu problem' and 'the Xhosa problem' (p. 87), and Van Jaarsveld discusses 'the Hottentot problem' (p. 117). Nowhere, however, is there any reference to a 'white problem', a 'settler problem', or a 'trekker problem' from the point of view of any non-white group, though it is obvious that the whites must have been at least as much of a problem to the blacks as the blacks were to the whites. The texts approach their subject-matter in this way because the framework of historical assumptions within which they are produced virtually precludes the possibility of viewing history in any alternative way.

The ethnocentrism of the books, however, does not lie merely in an unfortunate choice of phrases; it is far more fundamental, as a closer examination shows. If the texts are analysed in terms of the intentions, motives and goals attributed to the different parties, the differences in their treatment of different groups become apparent. Here we concentrate on a section of the syllabus headed 'British Policy in regard to the Hottentots, Slaves and Bantu'. In the case of Joubert's account of British Bantu policy up to 1834 in his Standard 8 text (pp. 87–90), the explanations offered for the actions of the British Government and its agents (including Cape governors and military commanders) is summarized below. This is our summary of the explanations given for British actions in the textbook by Joubert:

They sought to solve the 'Xhosa problem'. They were hesitant and indecisive. (Implicitly) the aim was the segregation of blacks and whites. British actions were constrained by financial problems caused by Napoleonic Wars and the Continental System. The Colonial Office was guided ('more often misguided') by the philanthropists. Caledon aimed to defend the Cape against possible attack by European powers; he also wanted to restore order on the frontier. Collins (a military commander) wanted to make peace with the Xhosa to avoid physical clashes. To retrieve cattle stolen by the Xhosa, Cradock introduced the 'spoor system';[1] other governors modified it. Somerset ('unfortunately') sided with Gaika against Ndlambe (it is not clear why). (Gaika and Ndlambe were Xhosa chiefs.) He settled British settlers to act as a buffer against the Xhosa. The British Government instructed D'Urban to make allies of the Xhosa.

The explanations offered for the actions of the philanthropists and missionaries are the following (our summary again):

They sought to influence British policy towards the Bantu, whom they saw as 'innocent children of nature' who needed protection against white exploitation. Dr Philip (of the London Missionary Society) sought to put the whites in the wrong over the Sixth Frontier War.

The actions of the colonists, Dutch and English, are explained as follows (our summary):

There was discontent and unrest among the whites on the frontier because they were dissatisfied with government policy. They hoped for compensation for their losses in the Sixth Frontier War. The Dutch-speaking colonists considered their welfare neglected by the British Government; they wanted to establish their own independent state.

The blacks, we are told, acted as they did for the following reasons:

The Xhosa saw vacillation of British policy as a sign of weakness. They marauded and thieved (motive implicit). There was a feud (unexplained) between Gaika and Ndlambe. Ndlambe invaded the colony out of revenge for Somerset's siding with Gaika.

---

1. Under the 'spoor system' the tracks of stolen cattle could be followed into Xhosa territory and the cattle retrieved.

It is easy to see that in this account of black–white relations on the frontier the whites are credited with complex, even conflicting, motives and goals and an attempt is made to explain their actions and interests in some depth. By contrast, very little attempt is made to explore the way the blacks behaved. They tend to be credited with very simple motivations (they were given to thieving, for instance) or alternatively their actions are left unexplained, even inexplicable. For instance, while the complicated relationships between the British Government, the different governors, the missionaries and philanthropists, and the English- and Dutch-speaking settlers are examined at length, the reader is given no idea of what Gaika and Ndlambe were feuding about. Similarly, though in the same chapter the British form of government and changing policies at the Cape are dealt with in detail, hardly any attention is given to forms of government among the Xhosa anywhere in the book, nor is it suggested that they might have anything resembling a 'policy' towards the whites. What the reader is offered is very much a white man's history of the period.

A very similar picture appears if the account given in the Van Jaarsveld text for the same section of the syllabus is analysed in the same way (pp. 124-32). His explanations for the actions of different groups are summarized in Appendix 6.

The most noticeable difference between this and the previous version is that Gaika and Ndlambe's feud and the Xhosa attack on the colony are made somewhat more intelligible. Even so, it is only necessary to point to the amount of space required to summarize the reasons given for white actions in comparison with that required for those of the blacks (21 lines for the whites, 5 for the blacks) to make it clear that this is a history of the whites in South Africa in which black interests and objectives are considered of little intrinsic importance.

The style of the third textbook, by Boyce, for the same part of the syllabus (pp. 116–20) does not lend itself so readily to this kind of analysis, for it makes fewer direct attributions of motive and intention, but instead often uses impersonal constructions: 'a shortage of land appeared', 'an invasion followed'. None the less, when the same approach is applied to this work the results bear out the general point made in the case of the other two books, as can be seen from Appendix 7.

The Boyce version has the distinction of making it clear that the farmers were sometimes the aggressors and not just the victims in their contacts with the Xhosa. The question of Boer culpability is glossed over by both the other texts. This and stylistic differences apart, however, the general picture is similar. This textbook, like the others, presents a history of the whites in which the blacks, though they are the majority group in South Africa, appear as rather crude cardboard cut-outs moving across the three-dimensional stage of white history. Implicitly these texts suggest to their readers that the blacks are only important in so far as they impinge on the interests of the whites.

So far we have relied mainly on one small though important section of the syllabus to illustrate a central characteristic of the history texts in use in South African schools. The white ethnocentrism we have described is a general feature of all the books we examined and could have been illustrated from almost any part of any of the texts dealing with South African history. It is present in books written specifically for blacks as well as in those for whites. In the black texts we examined the white ethnocentrism is somewhat attenuated by greater attention to the concerns and origins of the non-white groups, at least in Standard 8, as we saw in the previous chapter; but overall the history offered is still primarily a history of the whites.

Given the political and social circumstances of South African education, it is hardly surprising that this should be so. It is probable that some degree of ethnocentrism is to be found in the history teaching of any national education system, and in some cases there may even be gross distortion. It is still pertinent to ask whether the pattern we have outlined so far could be avoided. It can be argued, for instance, that the comparative lack of attention to the interests and motives of the blacks in the history books comes about because of a lack of historical source material, whereas detailed documentary sources exist for the whites. There is some force in this argument, but it is still true that less use is made of what source material exists than might be, and that the imbalance cannot be explained entirely on these grounds. This point can be illustrated with an example from the texts themselves.

A great deal is known about the tribal organization and customs of the various black groups but little of this is to be found in the history texts, even though on some occasions such information might go some way towards making historical events more intelligible. An example of more-than-usual attention to the circumstances of the blacks is to be found in the Standard 8 text for blacks by Van Rensburg, Schoeman and Vorster in the section dealing with the Mfecane (the period of turmoil and intertribal warfare between about 1815 and 1830). This section discusses the replacement of the small tribe as social unit by multi-tribal blocs, the adaptation of initiation ceremonies to military purposes among the Nguni, and the way the age-regiment system led to the widening of tribal loyalties, political centralization, and a shift of administrative power from traditional chiefs to commoners. This is very helpful in making the events of the period intelligible. No inkling of this sociological background, however, is given to the readers of the relevant sections of the Joubert, Van Jaarsveld or Boyce texts, nor even of the Mocke and Wallis (n.d.) Standard 8 text for black students. Yet it is only through the insights that this kind of information affords that students can be enabled to take the blacks seriously as peoples with a history and legitimate interests of their own. The book by Van Rensburg et al. shows that it is possible to go much further in this direction than is usual, even within the limitations of the syllabus. Clearly some of the characteristic shortcomings of the history books are due as much to a limited perspective as to lack of sources.

A further point that may be made about the texts in general is that not only are non-white concerns and aspirations devalued by neglect, but that at times the handling of non-white history amounts to actual trivialization. The Van Jaarsveld text, for instance, having previously referred to the Xhosa 'custom' of cattle rustling (p. 94) tells us that 'the Bantu often indulged in cattle rustling as a kind of "sport" and the whites did not understand this'. (p. 157). Equally trivializing is Podesta et al.'s (1976) opening statement about the customs of the Bushmen: 'The Bushmen were a cheerful, gay people who liked to dance' (p. 157). In Boyce (1974b) this stereotype of the happy childlike savage becomes that of the coloured person as a capering, grinning minstrel. The Standard 10 readers of this book are told; 'The coloured people are fond of sport, especially rugby, and of colourful and gay ceremonies such as the annual Coon Carnival in Cape Town. They are also endowed with a lively sense of humour' (p. 287). Boyce's Standard 6 book (1973a) says; 'The Xhosa were restless, however, resenting the loss of land' (p. 196). The phrase 'The Xhosa were restless' appears again on the next page. This is reminiscent of the old cliché from the popular literature and films of the British Empire, in which the District Commissioner's wife comments on the rising volume of drumbeats outside with: 'The natives are restless tonight.'

Racial difference

The aspect of the textbooks that we have considered so far is capable of serving an ideological role in the indirect sense that it implicitly confers greater legitimacy on white historical aims and concerns than on non-white ones. Other aspects of the books are more directly ideological in that they relate more explicitly to the idea of white supremacy and the philosophy of apartheid. This tendency is evident in the way that questions of racial difference and inequality are handled, in the way that parallels are drawn between the past and the present so as to make apartheid seem natural, and in the prevalence of some common assumptions of white folk wisdom that help to bolster the present system. We shall illustrate each of these in turn.

The defence of apartheid in terms of outright racism, that is of inherited physical differences between groups, is less common now than it used to be, particularly where the justification is intended for outside consumption. The official statements tend to stress ethnic differences and the need to preserve and foster the distinct cultural and national identities of each group. This formulation serves simultaneously to explain and legitimate Afrikaner nationalism itself as well as the goal of separate development for the non-white groups. By and large this approach is found in the history books also and crudely racist statements are uncommon. However, racist thinking is not far below the surface in some cases and every now and then it peeps through into the texts. Podesta et al.'s (1976) Standard 7 text for blacks provides an example. The readers are told that 'the Bushmen were a primitive race from the Stone Age who had been forced to leave Asia by a stronger race' (p. 157). The idea that is being conveyed here is that history may be explained by racial differences. The same assumption appears on the next page where we read that the Hottentots were stock farmers who had 'been pushed out by other races who were grain farmers' (p. 158). The use of the term 'race' as interchangeable with 'tribe' or 'ethnic group' entails an essentially racist conception, which is to be found also in Van Rensburg et al. when they talk of the whites and the Xhosa on the Eastern frontier as 'men of opposite races' (p. 102).

The most significant way that the underlying racism of the South African system is conveyed in the texts is in the sheer emphasis given to skin colour and racial differences, and in the use of the metaphor of 'mixing of blood' to describe miscegenation between racial groups. (The term 'interbreeding' in Van Jaarsveld's Standard 8 text appears as *bloedvermenging*—mixing of blood—in the Afrikaans original published a year earlier; there does not appear to be a suitable Afrikaans alternative.) The effect of the constant stress on physical differences is to leave the reader in no doubt that racial ancestry is of the utmost importance. Joubert's textbook tells us: 'The slaves from East Africa were Bantu; but those from Madagascar had a great deal of coloured blood in their veins. Those from the East were inhabitants of Java, Sumatra and Malaya.... Many of them also had lighter skins.... Hence, with the exception of those from East Africa, the slaves were "coloured"' (p. 81). In similar vein it describes the Griquas: 'In contrast to the Cape Coloureds, the Griquas had no slave blood in their veins. They were descendants of the Basters, Hottentots and Bushmen, with Hottentot blood predominant. Andries Waterboer, for example, had no white blood in his veins' (p. 82). Van Jaarsveld's text offers this astonishing piece of information: 'It was scientifically estimated in 1977 that the Coloured people of today are an admixture of 34 per cent white, 36 per cent indigenous and 30 per cent Asiatic blood' (p. 93). It is significant that such detail should be thought appropriate on this particular topic when it is frequently lacking on other topics. This passage also illustrates other general characteristics of the texts, namely, that sources of information are rarely acknowledged, and that contrary points of view are omitted. Thus in the present case the fact that the vast body of scientific opinion would regard the proportions of different ancestral 'blood', as such, as quite irrelevant to history is not mentioned.

Neither Mocke and Wallis (n.d.) nor Boyce show the same obsession with racial ancestry in their Standard 8 texts. Boyce's book simply notes that 'The origins of the Coloured People are to be found in the mixing of different racial groups such as Europeans, Hottentots, slaves and Bushmen'. It also points out that 'it is incorrect to think of the different groups as being classified into distinct types each with its own physical, language or economic characteristics' and inaccurate to think in terms of pure races (p. 107).

Inequality

The question of racial inequality arises in the texts in discussions of the British liberalization of laws relating to the Hottentots and slaves. Most texts stress the dissatisfaction of the farmers with these changes as one of the causes of the Great Trek. Generally it is quite clear that the author's sympathy lies with the farmers, while to avoid accusations of support for slavery there is usually a statement like this one from Van Jaarsveld: 'Seen in retrospect slavery is, of course, an inhuman practice but in those days people thought differently' (p. 92). The farmers' grievances are then detailed so uncritically that it is often difficult to distinguish between their views and those of the author. Even in Boyce, whose work is generally the least tendentious, it is not clear whether this view is his own or simply that of the colonists: 'The idea of equality between black and white introduced by humanitarians and missionaries was intolerable' (1973a, p. 163). The sympathetic presentation of the farmers' point of view in terms of present-day white South African attitudes allows them to appear as the injured parties and their reactions as entirely justified. Thus the Joubert text: 'The Ordinance introduced complete *equality* between Whites and Hottentots. The Whites were intensely indignant about the whole matter' (p. 86; italics in original).

The very idea of racial equality speaks for itself as a just cause for indignation. Joubert again: 'The owners of slaves could do nothing against the irritating regulations which they considered insulting' (p. 87). The serious purpose behind the regulations is effectively denied by describing them as 'irritating'. (The same word appears in Van Rensburg et al., p. 82.) Van Rensburg et al.'s textbook has this to say about the slave regulations on page 110:

Between 1816 and 1834 a series of proclamations were issued which made the farmer feel that he was no longer master on his own farm. His authority was undermined by the appointment of slave protectors, the registering of punishment and the stopping of work between 6 p.m. and 6 a.m. Slaves became cheeky.

Among white South Africans cheekiness is held to be a cardinal fault in a servant.

The whole tenor of the presentation in most books is such as to show the white stock-farmers in the best possible light, the regulations protecting slaves and Hottentots as unnecessary, and to avoid confronting the central question of why slavery and racial inequality should have been thought unacceptable. For instance, the inappropriateness of the slave regulations is underlined by pointing out that the anti-slavery lobby was mainly concerned with conditions in the West Indies, by comparison with which slaves at the Cape were well treated. Van Jaarsveld et al.'s (1974) Standard 6 book emphasizes this by including a rather harrowing picture of slaves being beaten in the West Indies. Similarly, the farmers are exonerated from supporting slavery as such: 'The people of the Cape were not opposed to the emancipation of slaves as such, but they were greatly inconvenienced and annoyed by the way in which it was implemented (p. 123). (The terms of compensation offered to the slave-owners were highly disadvantageous.) While the farmers' grievances are sympathetically handled, little effort is made to rehearse the arguments against slavery. The emancipation of the slaves is presented as a cause of the Great Trek: why the humanitarians should have been against slavery is barely considered. Only Paynter (n.d.) makes the telling point: '[Somerset] was accused of meddling in their [the farmers'] affairs, as they considered their slaves to be well treated. Of course, if this was so, they had no need to object to the new regulations' (Standard 6, p. 126). Also glossed over is why so many Hottentots took advantage of the new regulations to become vagrants rather than remain in white employment, for they too are said to have been well treated.

Parallels with the present

Another aspect of the texts that merits comment is the way that, in some of the books, parallels are drawn between the situation on the Eastern Cape frontier and present-day South Africa so as to suggest that apartheid is justified by history or that the present is just a natural development of the past. The use of the terminology of apartheid to describe historical events serves the same end. Today the infamous pass laws by which the movement, employment and right of abode of Africans are controlled are an important means by which apartheid is enforced. In 1809 Caledon had introduced a pass law for Hottentots; there had been some similar regulations under the Dutch. Caledon's law was repealed in 1828 and this became a grievance among the farmers, who complained that vagrancy and a shortage of labour resulted. According to Van Jaarsveld about 9,000 coloureds refused to work for the farmers once there was no law to compel them to. Further, after the slaves were freed 'many slaves left their previous employers and there was no Pass Law to control their movements' (p. 123). Later he tells us that both Governors Bourke and Cole 'allowed the Xhosa to cross the [Fish] river without passes' (p. 129) as part of their failure to enforce the policy of territorial separation. These statements are all made as though it is to be taken for granted that a pass law should form a normal part of any sensible policy. By implication the present-day pass laws are thereby made to seem unexceptionable.

The text for black schools by Van Rensburg et al. (pp. 79, 81), while pointing out that the law favoured the whites, also lists some benefits the law had for the Hottentots, such as teaching them good work habits. Its repeal entitled them to own land and

Above all, they were free to offer or withhold their labour and therefore to improve their condition through their right to leave bad masters and remain with good ones. The evil men among them were also free, naturally, to steal, cheat and trespass. The colonists immediately complained of the behaviour of these evil men. It soon became clear that many Hottentots had not yet reached the stage of development where they could appreciate and practise the political, economical and social rights which were given to them by Ordinance No 50.

Once again the pass system is supported and one of the legitimating ideas of the apartheid doctrine, the backwardness of the non-whites, is reinforced by appealing to the notion of 'stages of development'. Only groups that have reached a particular stage of development are thought to be entitled to civil rights.

National identity

The concept of 'national identity' is a key one in the philosophy of apartheid, for it is in the name of preserving and fostering the separate identities of the different population groups that segregation and exploitation are justified by the official apologists of the system. Van Jaarsveld uses the term mostly in connection with the Afrikaners, for his history of South Africa is essentially a history of the Afrikaners, whom he credits with a historic mission: 'Their task was to tame the wilderness and their only textbook was the Bible' (p. 90). This notion itself is part of the mythology of Afrikaner nationalism, and on page 85 of the Afrikaans version of Van Jaarsveld's (1973) book it is fleshed out as follows: *'Hulle het hul met Israel van ouds vergelyk—as "uitvekore" beskou en vervul met 'n "roeping"—', beskawingstaak in die land "Kanaan".'* (They compared themselves with Israel of old—as 'chosen' and charged with a 'mission'—a civilizing task in the land of Canaan.—Our translation.)

The biblical notion of a chosen people is no longer part of the official rhetoric, though many people still believe it, but the related concept of 'national identity' is quite central to apartheid doctrine, and Van Jaarsveld's readers are encouraged to think in these terms. Thus they are told, in a section headed 'National Identity', that at the time of the second British occupation the Dutch at the Cape already had their own national identity (p. 112), and that the Great Trek was an act of self-preservation, an attempt to retain their identity (pp. 114, 174). In similar vein, the Joubert text says that the Basters (a coloured group) had become an 'identifiable nation' by the middle of the eighteenth century. The way the idea is used to justify 'separate development' can be seen from Van Jaarsveld's treatment of Sir George Grey's policy in the Eastern Cape of 'civilizing' the Africans and treating them as equals (p. 224):

The Xhosa did not accept Grey's policy without reservations. There was opposition. The chiefs felt that their authority and influence was being undermined. Their condition might be compared with that of the Afrikaner in the Cape before the Great Trek. That which was peculiar to the Afrikaners was destroyed by the British with their policy of anglicization, and the reaction was the Great Trek: a rebellion against the British which took the form of leaving the country.

In similar fashion the Africans found themselves in opposition. They felt that that which was their own was being taken away from them....

The policy of the Voortrekkers in their Boer Republics was quite different. No equality was allowed in church or state, segregation was enforced and that which was peculiar to the African was left untouched. In their reserves, which were put aside for them, the African chiefs could rule their people according to their own laws and traditional administrative systems.

The text then goes on to add that 'the Voortrekkers certainly made use of African labour, and they tried to civilize and Christianize them in this way'. Such contradictions aside, however, the passage illustrates how, by means of the concept of national identity, of preserving 'that which is peculiar' to a group, the ideals of the Trekkers and the early Boer republics are implicitly transformed into a blueprint for the apartheid state, and in such a way that the Africans seem to be beneficiaries of the system.

The book by Van Rensburg and his co-authors offers a similar analysis based on the idea of national identity, though in a different context and with a black readership in mind. The Mfecane 'was a genuine process of nation-building, though in the course of its development it destroyed old unities as well as creating new ones' (p. 97). 'The memories and traditions of this period', it says, 'serve to maintain the sense of identity of peoples who were vitally affected by it' (p. 97). The missionaries had a westernizing influence on the Africans of the interior. 'However, the Black man's pride in his own identity limited their influence' (p. 100). White hunters, traders and farmers also had an influence, partly positive—adopting Western farming methods, clothing and food, for instance.

> But there were also negative influences on the life style of the Black man
> + detribalization which robbed them of identity;
> + moral decline as a result of strong drink and disruption of family life through migratory labour;
> + neglect of own home industries;
> + tobacco smoking became common.
>
> These more negative influences have stimulated a strong national feeling in the present day. This has resulted in the re-awakening of Black consciousness and a return to traditional values. Politically it gained expression in independent Black states in South Africa [p. 101].

For the authors to suggest to their black readers that what the modern Black Consciousness movement is really striving for is black homelands under apartheid is disingenuous to say the least. The passage provides an illustration of how the ideological use of the concept of national identity may descend into crude propaganda, but its use to justify apartheid closely parallels that of Van Jaarsveld.

Another tendency of some of the texts that is in accord with the ideology of apartheid is the way that segregation between the races is presented as the norm. On the eastern frontier in particular conflict between white and Bantu is frequently attributed to the failure of the British to enforce strict territorial segregation; 'weak' governors like Bourke and Cole are criticized for their lack of firmness, and D'Urban's conciliatory approach and Grey's 'civilizing' policy are represented as mistakes. The implicit message is that racial segregation is the only thing that works in a South African context.

Also noteworthy is the great stress placed in the textbooks by Joubert and Van Jaarsveld in particular on what has been called 'the myth of the empty land', the idea that the interior was uninhabited as a result of the Mfecane at the time the Trekkers moved in, and that this somehow gives the whites a greater entitlement to the land than the blacks. Historical research over the last fifteen years has shown that this is untrue, and that the territory was not nearly as uninhabited as the apologists of apartheid make out. What is important for our purposes is that this legitimating idea is given great stress and that there is no attempt to take account of contrary historical evidence. Both the Joubert and Van Jaarsveld books have maps to illustrate the emptiness of the interior; the book by Van Rensburg et al. makes the point, but not nearly so strongly; Boyce's text is careful to say only that the wars of the Mfecane 'facilitated the later extension of European settlement over this part of the interior of South Africa' (p. 141).

White folk wisdom

Something else that is worth illustrating is the way that certain common assumptions and stereotypes of white South Africa are appealed to and reinforced in the course of historical description. For instance, in discussions of Caledon's pass law and its repeal, to which we have already referred, there is commonly an appeal to the stereotype of the non-white as aimless, lazy, idle and work-shy. Thus the Joubert text tells us that Caledon 'was opposed to the vagrancy of some of the Hottentots as well as to their idleness at certain mission stations' (p. 85). One of the results of his proclamation is said to be that 'the Hottentots learnt to do *something useful*' (original italics). 'However, Caledon's proclamation had one defect; Hottentot children were still free to wander around, so Cradock introduced the apprentice system in 1812' (p. 85).

Another common piece of white folk wisdom is that outsiders do not understand (white) South African problems, that only by having continued contact with non-white people is it possible to understand what they are really like, and that ideas about equality dreamed up in Europe just do not apply in a South African context. This comes up repeatedly in the texts. Joubert writes: 'The missionaries and their philanthropic ideas were opposed by the colonists, whose views were based on years of experience and contact with the Non-Whites' (p. 84). And Van Jaarsveld and his co-authors tell his Standard 6 readers on page 164:

Philanthropists applied the French Revolutionary watchword 'Liberty, Equality, Fraternity' to *all* people regardless of colour, race or civilized attainment. In distant Europe they had no first-hand knowledge of the indigenous peoples of the colonies, but were dependent upon the reports of the missionaries.

This quotation also makes reference to two other popular beliefs that support the status quo. The first is that level of 'civilization' is the criterion by which civil rights should be allocated. This has come to replace for many whites the crude notion of racial inferiority. We saw an instance of it in an earlier quotation from Van Rensburg about the repeal of the pass law for Hottentots where the notion of 'stages of development' was invoked. The same idea appears in the Boyce text in support of a more positive conclusion: 'the Hottentots had been liberated from restrictions and as they became more civilized they formed a valuable part of the population of the colony' (p. 112). The Van Jaarsveld text likewise describes the frontier farmers' reaction to the new Hottentot regulations as follows: 'Their belief in differentiation, in a clear-cut master–servant relationship, seemed to have been swept aside by an Ordinance that apparently placed uncivilized people on the same footing as civilized people' (p. 177).

The other popular belief touched upon in the previous quotation from Van Jaarsveld is that humanitarian or liberal ideas are at best suspect, at worst dangerous. In some white South African circles the word 'liberal' is used almost interchangeably with 'communist'. The dismissal of liberal ideas—and they tend to be dismissed rather than argued against—tends to occur most frequently in respect of the activities of the philanthropists and missionaries, but it occurs elsewhere too. Boyce's book has this to say about Commissioner De Mist and Governor Janssens, the chief Dutch officials at the Cape during the Batavian period immediately preceding the second British occupation: 'Both men were firm believers in the principles of the French Revolution—liberty and equality—nevertheless they were practical men and able administrators' (p. 99). Why 'nevertheless'? Why should believers in equality not be practical and able? Van Rensburg et al. have almost the same thing: 'Liberals as they were, they nevertheless believed in strong government, and though much attracted by the ideas of equality and brotherhood, they were shrewd and practical men' (p. 61). In such ways are the concepts of the theoreticians of apartheid translated into the everyday common sense of South African whites.

Countering prejudices

A final criticism that can be made of most of the books has already been touched upon. Not only do they tend, in one way or another, to offer a worldview favourable to the continuance of the present system, but they frequently fail at appropriate points to counter common prejudices and historical myths. For instance, only in Boyce, as we have seen, is it pointed out that it is inaccurate to think of race as defining distinct types of human being. The other texts, where they do not actively encourage such thinking, make no effort to counter it; and, given the nature of South African society, crude racist thinking needs to be countered if it is not to persist by default. Here are two examples, both from Van Rensburg et al., of deliberate efforts to point out the limitations of previously accepted accounts in school history books. On page 70 they write:

In the past, in writings about frontier troubles, too much stress has been placed on mere cattle stealing, whereas the need for more grazing land for both Black and White, and the fundamental difference in their attitude to the holding of land, are the real causes of the conflict between them. African ideas about land were, moreover, similar to those of the White man's ideas [sic] about sea or air—in short, that it is something that can neither be bought nor sold.

Presumably this is as much a message to teachers brought up in the old school as to students. A similar message, with the book's black readership in mind, to teachers too heavily influenced by the Afrikaner view of history would seem to lie in the following passage on page 71:

It is a narrow view that sees in the 19th century only the White colonist, oppressed and misunderstood, fleeing into the wilderness to escape the tyranny of imperial power. Today we understand that it was necessary that an economic and social revolution should take place before a political revolution. Finally, whether welcome or not British rule introduced Southern Africa to new economic and political realities of the day and ideas of change.

Such attempts at correcting common misconceptions are however comparatively rare, except in the work of Boyce, which makes an effort to reformulate some of the received views of school history teaching in the light of new evidence. For example, he has this to say on page 142 about Mzilikazi, the Matabele chief:

Mzilikazi was a despotic ruler, but it would be inaccurate to regard him as only a bloody tyrant. He created a political community in which law and order prevailed. Many European visitors to Mzilikazi's kraals were favourably impressed by his government.

On a more central point, only in Boyce is it stated outright that the idea that the Trekkers entered an empty land is a myth. Though both Van Jaarsveld and Joubert refer to evidence that indicates black settlement in the interior long before the whites arrived, they still end up endorsing the myth of the empty land. Boyce, referring his readers to the *Oxford History of South Africa*, says unequivocally: 'Another myth, which has been dispelled by the study of the journals of ship-wrecked travellers—Portuguese, Dutch and English—is that the white settlers, as they moved inland, occupied an empty land' (p. 107). Later, on page 136, the same text is even more forthright in undermining the received wisdom of most textbooks:

It is one of the legends in South African history that these Bantu people were newcomers to South Africa, in fact there are school history books which still give the impression that the Bantu arrived in South Africa about the same time as the white colonists were moving towards the eastern frontier of the Cape Colony. Recent research, however, shows that the earliest Bantu invaders from the north may have reached southern Africa as early as the eleventh or twelfth centuries A.D.

Only an approach that is actively critical of these historical myths and the prevalent racist assumptions of South African society can redeem school history from its present ideological role.

The overall conclusion to be drawn from an examination of the material considered in this chapter is that, in spite of a few attempts to correct some traditional biases of South African history teaching, the textbooks tend to present a view of the past consistent with and generally supportive of current South African racial politics. The accounts offered of relations between black and white in the first part of the nineteenth century are generally crude and misleading, value judgements are frequently presented as fact, inconvenient facts ignored, and evidence is not discussed. In these respects, the texts, in presenting a very partial 'white man's view' of history, fail to match up even to the objectives laid down in the Transvaal Education Department's history syllabus, particularly the aim: 'To educate to an objective approach towards history, fostering the habit of first investigating all relevant facts before passing judgement' (Item 3.9).

6 South African contemporary history

Introduction

In the previous chapter we illustrated characteristic ways in which history textbooks in use in South African secondary schools tend to support the ideology of white supremacy in their treatment of nineteenth-century history. In this chapter we focus on interpretations of twentieth-century South African history. We examine three textbooks written for the Standard 10 history syllabus. Standard 10 history covers the period 1919–70 and this constitutes the content for the matriculation or school-leaving examination.

As with the previous chapter, we examine the presentation of different ethnic groups to determine how far, and in what context, a white-centred approach to history may be evident. At the same time, we have sought to establish whether or not particular ideological perspectives form part of these interpretations. One way of approaching this is to see how the texts deal with instances of conflict and political dissent.

The textbooks selected for this analysis include the two texts approved by the Transvaal Education Department. One of these is a translation from Afrikaans of the text by C. J. Joubert (1979), *History for Standard 10*; the other, written in English, is *Europe and South Africa*, Part 2, by A. N. Boyce (1974*b*). The third textbook is by A. P. J. van Rensburg and J. Schoeman—*Active History, Standard 10* (1980*b*)—and is written specifically for the black education system.

We start out by examining the structure of the Standard 10 South African history syllabus, since this has largely determined the structure of the texts themselves. Table 19 shows the syllabus outline, together with the proportion of space allocated to topics in the three textbooks.

The main point that needs to be made about the structure of the syllabus is that the recent history of the white and the non-white groups is defined in terms of 'development' and is treated in segregated sections, implying that they have developed separately. The non-white section is also divided into three compartments: Bantu, Indian and coloured. This division is, in reality, an artificial one since constant interaction has occurred between the different population groups.

TABLE 19. Standard 10: South African history syllabus (percentages)

	Joubert	Boyce	Van Rensburg/Schoeman
Political development	14.2	21.6	27.0
Constitutional development	15.7	12.3	18.1
Economic and social development	19.8	21.4	15.0
Development of non-white peoples	30.3	20.1	18.9
South Africa's external policy	20.1	24.5	20.8
TOTAL[1]	100.1	99.9	99.8

1. Totals do not add up to exactly 100 per cent due to rounding.

Although not explicitly defined in the syllabus, the texts also reveal a distinction in the time period covered by white and non-white history. In this respect white history is given prominence until the late 1940s when the National Party came to power. At this point, non-white people become the focus of attention. It appears that the switch from one group to the others here is by no means accidental. It is almost as though white history reached its apotheosis with the election of the Nationalist government, and that the residual political problems concerned how to deal with the blacks. This is borne out by a passage in the 1980 Van Rensburg and Schoeman text, which in the introduction to 'Non-white Development' (p. 140) states:

Whereas the previous [syllabus] units were dominated by relations between Afrikaans and English-speaking South Africans, the future place of Non-Whites in South African society became the main issue after the end of World War II. The South African community as a whole had been affected by this problem over the past three decades, while world opinion has focused sharply on our country.

The above quotation illustrates again how the history is presented from a white perspective, even in a textbook written for black education. The division made between white and non-white history in terms of a time perspective is also artificial. Relations between whites and non-whites were significant issues well before 1948, as we saw in the previous chapter. The period after 1948 merely saw the formalization and extension in policy and ideology of already well-established practices to maintain the existing socio-political hierarchy.

Table 19 shows that only 30, 20 and 19 per cent of the three texts respectively are given to 'The Development of the Non-white Peoples'. The Van Rensburg and Schoeman text, written specifically for blacks, gives the lowest proportion of all to this topic.

Political history

This portion of the analysis examines the presentation of white groups in twentieth-century political history, as defined in the syllabus topics 'The Political Development of South Africa' and 'The Constitutional Development of South Africa'. Reference is made to the presentation of other ethnic groups in the texts, where this is appropriate.

It will be useful to touch briefly on some historiographical points which are relevant to the texts. It has been noted in Chapter 2 that the majority of textbooks examined in our analyses conform to what Van Jaarsveld has termed *The Afrikaner's Interpretation of South African History* (Van Jaarsveld, 1964). This school of thought, we indicated, arose as a reaction to the British colonial perspective which dominated historical writing in the nineteenth century. The difference between the two is epitomized by the fact that what is still known in English as the Anglo-Boer War, or simply the Boer War, is called in Afrikaans the *Vryheidsoorlog*—the War of Independence (literally, 'of freedom').

The Afrikaner interpretation of history, we observed, is characterized by a polemical approach which stresses the role of Afrikaner heroes, gives peripheral treatment to other groups (white and non-white) and focuses heavily on political events. We also noted that a number of myths grew out of this writing which have been perpetuated to the present day. These myths concern, among other things, the rise of Afrikaner nationalism, the practice of racial segregation and the policy of separate development.

The Joubert and the Van Rensburg and Schoeman texts conform fairly closely to this school of thought. In particular, they focus heavily on the role of Afrikaner groups at the expense of other groups (white and black) and the mythology of Afrikaner nationalism permeates their texts. The text by Boyce, on the other hand, gives more attention to the English-speaking and black groups than the other two.

The syllabus around which these texts are based starts in 1910 with the formation of the Union of South Africa, when the two former Boer republics (the Transvaal and Orange Free State) combined with the two former British colonies (the Cape and Natal). At this time South Africa became a self-governing dominion within the British Empire. The textbooks then trace the rise of political parties and examine the policies of different governments and opposition groups, with much emphasis placed on the personalities of political figures during the period.

The interpretations offered are primarily concerned with the attempts of various Afrikaans-speaking groups to attain political power, cultural recognition and the loosening of ties with Great Britain. They are also concerned, to a lesser extent, with what they see as the political tension between the white Afrikaans and English-speaking groups.

The texts start out by focusing on tension between Afrikaans-speaking and English-speaking groups at the time of Union eight years after the end of the Anglo-Boer War. This, according to the narratives, was complicated by intergroup conflict among Afrikaners themselves over relations with Great Britain. The Afrikaners are initially portrayed as divided into strong anti-British factions, on the one hand, seeking to relinquish all association with the former colonial power, and groups more pragmatic in their policies towards Great Britain on the other. We are told that the anti-British groups wished to promote a specific Afrikaner cultural identity in reaction to the colonial legacy, and were the forerunners of the Afrikaner nationalist movement which increasingly dominated the South African political scene in the 1930s. This all culminated in the election, in 1948, of the present ruling National Party.

The analysis that follows focuses on three aspects of these interpretations: first, the emphasis given to Afrikaner cultural identity during the period; second, the role and nature of dissent among white groups; and third, the presentation of non-Afrikaner groups.

AFRIKANER IDENTITY

The promotion of an Afrikaner cultural identity arose initially as a reaction to British colonial influence in South Africa. One of the chief advocates of this cause was Hertzog, who led the opposition to South Africa's first premier, Botha, and was himself Prime Minister from 1924 to 1938. As a champion of Afrikaner rights, Hertzog introduced Afrikaans as an official language.

Underlying this notion of an Afrikaner *cultural* identity in two of our texts (Joubert, and Van Rensburg and Schoeman) are the wider and more all-embracing concepts of Afrikaner *national* identity and Afrikaner nationalism itself. This can be seen in the Van Rensburg and Schoeman narrative (1980, pp. 145–6) that discusses Hertzog's ideal for the Afrikaner people:

[Hertzog] was determined that Afrikaner nationalism should not die. He strove to lift his people up from the despondency into which they had sunk and to rid them of the sense of inferiority that had settled upon them.... He insisted only on an equality of rights which alone could ensure the survival of the Afrikaner people. This was also the basis of his two-stream policy which he defined as 'two nationalities, each flowing in separate channels'. Hertzog thought that Botha's one-stream policy might eventually lead to the destruction of the Afrikaner nation and that the Dutch language could also be destroyed by the far stronger English culture.

This transmutation of a culture into a nation is an important notion because it forms part of the Afrikaner mythology upon which the rhetoric of apartheid is based. In this context, apologists of apartheid reason that each tribal group should be regarded as a separate cultural and national entity and given its own homeland to preserve its national identity. It is worth reproducing a brief quote from the 1979 Joubert text, where Hertzog's philosophy is discussed. The similarity between this passage (p. 163) and contemporary rhetoric is self-evident:

[Hertzog] saw each population group as a separate stream, each having its own language and culture, each with a right to separate existence. But each would combine with the other in building the country.

The Afrikaner national ideal, which was to pave the way for future apartheid policy, was resurrected in the 1930s when it took on a more overtly political tone in the form of what the texts call the republican ideal, or republicanism. At this time, another split occurred in the Afrikaner political ranks when Hertzog, the early proponent of Afrikaner rights, was challenged over his 'moderate' policy *vis-à-vis* Great Britain. The new hero of Afrikaner nationalism was Malan, who founded, in opposition to Hertzog, the 'purified' Nationalist Party. Malan proposed the severing of all ties with Great Britain and the setting up of a South African Republic. It was he who won the 1948 election on a platform devoted to the republican ideal and the policy of apartheid.

It is interesting to compare the treatment accorded in the three textbooks to the events that were part of the revival of Afrikaner nationalism. One such event was the symbolic re-enactment of the Great Trek, which took place in a fervour of religious patriotism and hero worship. The impression gained from reading one of the texts (Van Rensburg and Schoeman, 1980*b*) is that the 'fervour' of this event still remains, as we read, for example, that 'it brought all Afrikaners under the influence of their historic past'; 'it made Afrikaners aware of their common heritage'; and that it was 'the unique event in the history of the Afrikaners' (p. 171).

This is not, however, the case in all the books. Boyce's text is considerably more distanced from the event: 'The Voortrekker centenary celebrations of 1938 provided Malan's party with that emotional impulse which the United Party lacked' (Boyce, 1974b, p. 232). This textbook also is the only one that makes reference to Malan's speech at this event where he stated that 'the white man was facing the black man at a new battle of Blood River, but this time he had to fight for his life on the open plains of economic competition' (Hancock, 1962, p. 289, cited in Boyce, 1974b, p. 232). Thus only from the Boyce textbook does the reader have any hint of the broader dimensions of this nationalistic movement, particularly the ideal of white domination.

AFRIKANER DISSENT

We now go on to look at interpretations of dissent among the white groups, focusing on one historical event, a rebellion, as an extreme example of Afrikaner dissent. At the outbreak of the First World War in 1914, Britain called upon South Africa to invade German South West Africa. Botha agreed to this request but the move was opposed by those Afrikaners who espoused the anti-British cause. A rebellion then ensued, led by veteran Anglo-Boer War leaders, which was subsequently squashed by forces loyal to the Botha government.

It is interesting to see how this event is dealt with since it unequivocally represented a form of direct dissent against the government of the time. While not explicitly condoning the rebel cause, the texts do attempt to locate it in the context of prevailing sentiment. For example, in Van Rensburg and Schoeman (1980b, p. 150) we read:

Twelve years had not been enough to wipe out the resentment and distrust of generations which had culminated in the Anglo-Boer War. Many Afrikaners saw the war as another episode in the old struggle for independence.

In locating the rebellion in this context, it then becomes 'more of a spontaneous expression of feeling than a revolt' (p. 151). Joubert's book similarly states that the initial phase of the rebellion 'may thus be seen as a kind of armed protest' (1979, p. 165). The rebellion of 1916 is implicitly vindicated later in the Van Rensburg and Schoeman text (p. 170), when it becomes associated with the Afrikaner republican ideal:

Apart from being a protest against the Botha government's policy to invade South West Africa, the Rebellion of 1914–15 was also a Boer revolt aimed at recovering republican independence. The Rebellion failed miserably. But one result of this was that the Afrikaner now decided on constitutional methods rather than force to restore the republic.

There are two points to be made here. Firstly, where previously the text spoke of 'many Afrikaners' having nationalist sentiments (previous quotation), it now refers to 'the Afrikaner', as though the nationalist movement had the unanimous support of Afrikaners, which it did not. In both Van Rensburg and Schoeman and Joubert, there is a tendency to see the history of South Africa as the history of the Afrikaners, and for the history of the Afrikaners to become identified with the history of Afrikaner nationalism. Secondly, while these texts present Afrikaner political dissent as an expression of legitimate political sentiment, as we shall see later, black dissent is characteristically attributed to illegitimate external forces.

NON-AFRIKANER GROUPS

We now examine the presentation of non-Afrikaner groups in contemporary political history, starting with an examination of the English-speaking white group. In general, the motives and interests of this group tend to be underplayed, particularly in the Joubert and Van Rensburg/Schoeman narratives. There is also a tendency to present the English-speakers in over-generalized terms as pro-imperialist and anti-Hertzog. By comparison with the Afrikaner group, the English-speaking group receive little attention other than where they appear to impinge on Afrikaner interests. Thus they tend to receive most attention from the authors at the beginning of the period when the tension between the two white groups is said to have been at its peak.

It will be instructive to examine a case where the interests of the two groups are seen to be in conflict. The case in question concerns the English-speaking group's attitude towards Hertzog prior to the 1910 election, when this group feared that Hertzog's inclusion in the Botha cabinet would threaten their interests. In only one of the three textbooks, Boyce (1974b, pp. 210–11), is any attempt made to explore what these interests were:

> [Hertzog's] policies and influence were viewed with alarm by many, especially the English-speaking electorate. It was his Education Act, applied in the Free State, based on the principles of compulsory bilingualism in the teaching of Dutch and English and the use of both languages as media of instruction which was resented most, because it was feared that it would be extended to the other provinces.
>
> Hertzog, in one of his early election speeches, had expressed his conviction that South Africa should be ruled by Afrikaners, but he had also explained that by Afrikaners he meant all English- and Afrikaans-speaking persons who regarded South Africa as their fatherland.

By contrast, in Joubert there is no reference to the election speech noted above and in discussing Hertzog's Education Act the text states only that 'Afrikaners had accepted this, but English-speaking South Africans had generally condemned it. Hertzogism—as they referred to Hertzog's policy—was nothing but an attempt to protect the Afrikaner's identity' (Joubert, 1979, p. 164).

The syllabus is structured in such a way that white and non-white contemporary history is treated separately. As was pointed out earlier, the division is a highly artificial one, and in the nature of things our texts have all, to a greater or lesser extent, had to make reference to black groups in their treatment of 'white' political history. The tendency noted in the previous chapter for the Standard 8 texts to treat the blacks as a 'problem' is also present in the Standard 10 books. The same white-centred perspective is apparent in the tendency to treat the interests of blacks as necessarily subordinate to those of whites.

An example of this concerns a strike by white mine-workers which occurred in 1922 during an economic depression. The strike arose when the Chamber of Mines decided to reduce labour costs by employing more non-whites in semi-skilled work at lower wages. When the strike became violent, the Prime Minister (General Smuts) declared martial law and used armed force to quell the disturbances.

In the texts it appears to be taken for granted that the interests of white miners should be regarded as paramount. While the whites are presented as victims of poverty and unscrupulous labour practices the lowly position of the blacks is accepted without question. In Boyce (1974b, p. 223), for example, we are told that the mine-owners' decision 'threatened the security of the landless and poor Afrikaners who had flocked to the Witwatersrand and were incapable of doing skilled work'. But no mention is made of the poverty of black mine-workers who found themselves in a similar position—instead they become a problem to the white miners.

The black group only receive attention in the Van Rensburg and Schoeman text in so far as they are seen as a security threat. In this respect the reader learns: 'an extremely dangerous situation could develop if thousands of black workers should find themselves suddenly idle as a result of the strike by white workers' (1980, p. 158). The idea of white precedence is further reinforced in this text when we learn that the strike represented 'a big set-back to the white mine-workers'.

Economic and social history

The topics specified in the section of the syllabus entitled 'Economic and Social Development' are outlined in Table 20, together with the proportion of space allocated to them by our three authors.

TABLE 20. Economic and social development (Section 3 of Standard 10 South African history syllabus)

Topic	Boyce	Joubert	Van Rensburg
Great Depression	—	3.2	1,9
Poor white problem	2.5	2.7	2.5
Mining and industries	13.1	6.5	3.2
White and non-white labour	4.3	1.9	1.9
Urbanization (black and white)	1.5	5.5	4.9
Percentage of total	21.4[1]	19.8	15.0[1]

1. Includes additional material not specified in syllabus.

Although this section of the syllabus is clearly intended to present a history of the white groups in South Africa, the texts have been unable to segregate white and non-white social and economic history as neatly as was done with political history. There is thus considerable reference to non-white groups as well as to whites. The three authors all treat the topic differently.

The dominant feature of Joubert's (1979) text is its emphasis on a fixed socio-economic hierarchy based on a racial division of labour. This hierarchy is ascribed to historical as well as perceived 'natural' causes, and the interpretation becomes an explicit legitimation of the South African social structure. Nowhere is this assumption of a natural social order more explicit than in the claim (p. 232) that South Africa has never had a white working class and that this role has always been played by the non-white group:

South Africa has never actually had a White working class, as is the case in European countries. From the early days of the White settlement in this country, Non-Whites have been the labourers and because of a chronic shortage of labour in the Cape, governors soon had to import slaves. Detribalised Hottentots were later absorbed into the labour force, and over the years it became the accepted thing for Non-Whites to do all the heavy work. This was how a Non-White working class developed. Whites came into contact with the Blacks in about 1770 when the boundaries of the Cape were extended. In due course, White farmers in remote frontier areas started to engage Blacks as labourers, and like the Coloureds, they did only the heavy work and simple jobs.

After the interior had been opened up by the Voortrekkers, the Blacks remained the labourer [sic]. In this way a division of labour based on race came into being in South Africa, with the Blacks as labourer in the employ of the White man.

The first point which needs to be made regarding the claim that there has never been a white working class is that it is not only untrue but contradicts an earlier statement in the text concerning urbanization: 'The Afrikaner played an inferior part in the Country's economy for many years. He remained a member of the working class' (p. 226). More important, by omitting all reference to *how* the racial division of labour arose, the text suggests that it followed a natural course. We are told in this respect that it became the 'accepted thing' for non-whites to do all the heavy work. What we are not told about are the factors which drove non-whites to the workplace or the legislation that promoted and sustained this social order.

It is useful to examine how the Joubert text rationalizes the social structure. It first suggests that non-whites made their labour freely available: 'The presence of large numbers of Non-Whites who were prepared to offer their services cheaply made it unnecessary for the Whites to undertake arduous labour' (p. 232). In this argument a picture is evoked of non-whites eagerly queueing up for employment, content to receive a subsistance wage. What the reader is not told is why non-whites 'offered their services cheaply'. Nowhere in this account is there any mention of the coercion of labour through taxation and through the dispossession of land and livelihood. Moreover, the text then suggests that this social order was acceptable to the non-whites, though no evidence is presented for this view. Instead, the acceptability of inferiority is attributed to a simple form of materialism: 'The generally possessionless Non-White respected the White with his possessions. The Non-White did not therefore regard it as strange to find himself in an inferior position' (p. 232). This highly paternalistic interpretation once more obscures the insidious aspects of labour coercion referred to above.

Having firmly located the non-white group in the social structure, this textbook then turns to the role of the white group: 'The young pioneer was able to find land for himself to start an independent life of his own, until well into the 19th Century. He never found it necessary to start out life as a labourer' (p. 232). What is not explained here is that in the course of 'finding land for himself' the white pioneer contributed to the presence of large numbers of non-whites 'offering their services cheaply'. Nor is it explained that laws were passed to define the white groups' role in the economy. For example, the Mines and Works Act of 1911 forbade the employment of blacks as skilled workers in mines, while Hertzog's so-called 'civilized' labour policy was expressly directed at protecting the white worker. This, as much as anything else, condemned the non-white groups to the lower end of the social scale. While these policies are referred to elsewhere in the text, they are not introduced into the discussion of the historical determinants of a social order based on a non-white working class.

One of the dominant assumptions underlying the Joubert text's interpretation is that this social order was and remains in accord with a common consensus of both blacks and whites. The suggestion is also that, while it was acceptable for the non-white groups to be at the lower end of the social scale, it was and is not acceptable for white groups.

The same assumption is implicit in this textbook's interpretation of what is commonly referred to as the 'poor white problem'. The term is used to describe the pauperization of rural Afrikaners who migrated to the urban areas and were forced to compete in the labour market with unskilled black workers. It is, incidentally, worthy of note here that no mention is ever made of a 'poor black problem', despite their lowly position in the socio-economic order. The assumption here is that this was not a 'problem', and reflects the underlying value that black poverty is natural and not to be questioned (p. 215):

> The destitute farmer who migrated to the city found that he had to compete as an unskilled worker with the Non-White. The Non-White with his considerably lower standard of living, was prepared to work for wages much lower than the White could accept.

In appealing to the notion of consensus and by drawing on a highly partial view of history, the textbook constructs a thesis of a fixed social order. This thesis is then extended to legitimate implicitly the present order, to suggest that economic differences between groups result from differences in entitlement, that the way things are is broadly the way they should be. This is exemplified in the discussion of factors which stimulated economic growth after the Second World War. One such factor, the reader is told, lies in a convenient division of labour: 'The White population has both the initiative and the education to undertake and administer new enterprises. The very large Non-White population is not only a source of unskilled labour, but is also a huge market' (p. 223).

The second Transvaal text, by Boyce, approaches the section on 'Economic and Social Development' with an entirely different perspective. The most obvious difference is that it is far less tied to the ideology of apartheid. While it presents a more critical interpretation of the subject, there is also an apparent reluctance to enter too far into a subject which by any standard must be considered controversial.

The textbook by Boyce (1974b) avoids the compartmentalization, or 'textbook apartheid' which the syllabus suggests. The section on 'Urbanization', for example, does not deal with black and white groups separately but gives an integrated account which attempts to draw parallels between the two groups. In this brief account we learn that one of the causes of black urban migration was the Land Act of 1913 which had the effect of pushing them off the land, because it restricted the sale of land to blacks and forced them to work for white farmers. We also learn that the blacks were pushed off the land to seek wage employment to pay taxes. This interpretation contrasts with the simplistic notion of blacks being 'prepared to offer their services cheaply' put forward in the Joubert text. Boyce's textbook also mentions the negative aspects of black urban migration, explaining that it has deprived, and continues to deprive, the rural areas of much-needed young adult males, that it causes social dislocation, and that temporary employment makes it difficult for black labourers to acquire skills and thus has the effect of perpetuating poverty. On page 253 it is also pointed out that

> as long as workers are unskilled, and the continued existence of the colour bar in South Africa has this effect, employers will find that they do not lose a great deal through a big turnover of labour. Thus the migratory labour system is not considered to be a disadvantage because wages can be kept low; but if labourers began to do skilled work, the cost of a high turnover of labour would rise substantially.

While this textbook's interpretation of black urbanization and labour is in itself well balanced in the sense that it examines underlying causes and attempts to provide a black perspective on issues, it does at the same time underplay other matters. For example, we are told in passing that it has been the policy of the South African Government to 'discourage the permanent urban settlement of Bantu' (p. 253), but there is no attempt to explain this policy or examine its consequences. (A brief, mostly factual account is given in the section on 'Separate Development'.) Thus the reader is not enlightened on other pernicious conditions associated with black urban settlement, such as segregation, poor housing, destruction of squatter areas, pass laws and forced repatriation to so-called black states.

In its treatment of the 'poor white problem' the Boyce text implies that it is acceptable to be a poor black but not a poor white. On page 259 it states:

The government of the period 1924–33 felt strongly that the poverty of the poor whites had to be attended to, not only because they possessed the parliamentary vote but because their poverty was considered to be degrading to the white man.

Where Joubert says that wages were 'lower than the White *could* accept', Boyce makes it clear that poverty was only '*considered* to be degrading to the white man' (our italics). What in Joubert appears as inevitable, even natural, in Boyce is historically contingent. Where Joubert seems to suggest, 'This is the way things are, and should be,' Boyce is content to say, 'This is the way things turned out.' The difference is important.

The third textbook in our sample, Van Rensburg and Schoeman (1980*b*), more closely resembles Joubert in its interpretation of 'Economic and Social Development', although it is less explicitly ideological. Because it has been written for the black education system, there is evidence that more effort has been made to include a black perspective. Nevertheless, it still remains an essentially white interpretation and is characterized by a failure to give adequate explanation to the underlying causes of such phenomena as urban migration. There is also an implicit notion of a natural social order based on a racial division of labour, which can be seen in the interpretation of the 'poor white problem': 'The Poor White worker, himself unskilled, thus found that in unskilled ranks, preference was given to the Black worker who could afford to work for a far lower wage than the White worker' (p. 189). By suggesting that the black worker could *afford* to work for a lower wage than the white worker, as in Joubert, the text implies that a low standard of living was acceptable for blacks but not for whites.

It is interesting, also, to compare the treatment accorded to black and white migrants to the urban centres. More text is devoted to the poor white migrant, and the pathos of the poor white Afrikaaner is strongly evoked, by focusing on his 'loss of identity' and 'humiliation'. By contrast, the plight of the black migrant is considerably underplayed. While we are told that he became 'detribalized', nothing is said about any corresponding loss of identity or humiliation.

A further characteristic of this text is the tendency to oversimplify historical processes and underplay causal factors. Nowhere is this more explicit than in its interpretation of black urbanization: 'The urbanization of the Black man was the result of a twofold process—rural poverty drove him from his tribal territory [and] the city with its glitter and fascination attracted him' (p. 193).

This is a simplification of the 'push–pull' thesis which identifies the process of rural–urban migration in terms of factors that cause the migrant to leave and those that attract him at the other end. This idea is used in the text to examine, albeit briefly, what some of these push–pull factors were. In examining the 'pull' factor we are told on page 194 that:

Contact with Western civilization had created a demand for goods—especially clothes, blankets, food, liquor, household and agricultural implements. Therefore there was a need for cash income.
   Living in the city further stimulated the Black man's taste for Western goods which soon came to be regarded as a status symbol. And so migration from the homelands to the cities became a chain reaction.

Such explanations, in addition to oversimplifying and trivializing a complex social process, also obscure the more insidious factors which caused black migration. Nowhere in this interpretation is there any reference to taxation as a factor which drove blacks off the reserves to seek a cash income. Instead, the explanation is reduced to a simple form of materialism which then becomes a 'status symbol'.
   In a similar way, we learn that 'primitive methods of cultivation' resulted in land degradation and caused people to leave the reserves. While decline in agricultural productivity certainly has been a cause in the migration process, no mention is made of the Land Act of 1913 which had the effect of restricting the sale of land to blacks. Thus, rather than focusing on the limitations imposed on farming systems through pressure on land and resources, we are simply told that the problem lay in 'primitive methods of cultivation'.

Apartheid

This portion of the analysis looks at the syllabus section entitled 'Political, Social and Constitutional Development of the Non-white People'. The topics specified under this heading are shown in Table 21, together with the space allocated by the three textbooks in our sample.

TABLE 21. Political, social and constitutional development of the non-white people (percentages)

Topic	Joubert	Boyce[1]	Van Rensburg
Bantu	51	30	56
Indians	28	20	21
Coloureds	21	25	23

1. Text includes additional material not specified in syllabus.

THE BLACKS

Joubert (1979) devotes twenty pages of text to the blacks from 1910 onwards, over half of which is devoted to the topic of 'Separate Development', with much of this relating to current issues. What is presented, however, is not so much black history as a history of legislation, sponsored by whites, to control the lives of blacks. From the outset of Joubert's text, this white-centred perspective dominates. His opening sentence reads: 'The population ratio between Blacks and Whites was 4:1 in 1910 which alone made the Black–White relationship a countrywide problem and encouraged Whites to move towards Union' (p. 238).

In the first two paragraphs alone, there are no less than six references to this 'problem' without any clear definition of what it is. The only clue given is the numerical disparity between the groups and a vague notion of the white need to impose some kind of control or, as it is put, to 'formulate a national Black policy'.

There then follows a section on black political development that outlines the various pieces of legislation introduced during the period, which defined the black group's status within South African society. The remainder of the text is confined to the explication of apartheid, with occasional glimpses back into history where this serves to reinforce arguments that relate to present policy.

For example, the section 'Administration of the Blacks' asks why a separate administrative system is necessary and on page 241 provides the following white-centred and paternalistic answer:

Ever since the earliest days the Whites had regarded themselves as guardians to the Blacks, and it was their task to lead the Black man to help him develop and to protect his interests. This guardianship could best be pursued by means of a separate administrative system.

This historical argument is used to justify what are stated to be continuing reasons for this separate administration. The ethnocentrism evident above continues as we read (p. 241):

The Blacks differ from the Whites socially and economically. This difference is best recognized in a separate administrative system. Because the Black's level of achievement is lower than the White's in several fields (education, economic, social life), it would be unreasonable to administer him in the same way as the White person is administered.

Later in the text it is stated that a separate administration is there 'to protect the interest, promote the welfare, and guide the development of the Blacks in a desirable direction' (p. 243). It is taken for granted that the 'desirable direction' is the direction considered by the whites to be desirable for the blacks. Notice also that educational and economic disparities between white and black are presented simply as disparities in achievement rather than mostly the result of disparities in opportunity and provision.

Similar historical justification also occurs in Joubert's preamble to the section on 'Separate Development', on page 245. Here the origin of black territorial settlement is explained by the 'empty land' thesis, which, as we have seen elsewhere in this report, is now widely contested.

In Standard Eight you learnt how the Difaqane[1] was responsible for the depopulation of large areas of the interior and how the Voortrekkers settled in these areas. The areas where surviving Blacks lived became known as locations or reserves.

This neat, unambiguous historical explanation provides the setting for later apartheid rhetoric. For example, on page 247 he writes (our italics):

---

1. Also called the Mfecane—the period of intertribal warfare and devastation between about 1815 and 1830.

The established nationhood of the Whites has to be protected and maintained in that part of the country that *has always been theirs*. At the same time, the policy provides for the development of each separate Black nation to full autonomy. The focal point of this development is the Black States. These states are those parts of the country that *originally belonged* to the Blacks and still belong to them.

Part of the rationale for separate 'national' development is derived from the notion of national identity, as we have already observed. From this the notion of 'ethnic national identity' is derived: the black people, like the Afrikaners, can be given a national identity and homeland to go with it. Having given them this identity, the next logical step is to regard each separate group as a nation.

It is instructive to see how the text deals with the relationship between national identity and nation in the context of apartheid policy (pp. 246–7):

The population of South Africa has never been homogeneous. The Whites wish to retain their national identity in their own territory. At the same time, it must be acknowledged that Black peoples also wish to assert their national identities. History has shown that each nationalism cannot be artificially grafted on to another. Up to that time events in Africa, particularly in the former Central African Federation have shown that it is difficult to include both White and Black in one political system. It would be foolhardy to try to repeat the experiment in South Africa. The Black man of Africa refuses to become a 'semi-European'. He insists on Africanization—on the expression of his group aspiration. If all the different population groups of South Africa were included in one system, one or more groups would inevitably dominate the others.

This quotation is an example of an interpretation presented as though it were a fact, and it illustrates some of the assumptions upon which the interpretation is based. Why, for instance, should the merging of two nationalisms necessarily be 'artificial'? Why must 'the Black man' either become a 'semi-European' (and why 'semi'?), or follow the path of separate development? Are there no other alternatives? And why is it 'inevitable' that one or more groups will dominate the others? No explanation or evidence is offered in support of any of these assumptions, apart from the reference to the Central African Federation (now Malawi, Zambia and Zimbabwe).

White domination is thus defended as a means of preventing one group from dominating others, and the present system is represented as being in some way beneficial to black people, and in accordance with their alleged aspirations. This text's treatment of post-colonial African history is examined more thoroughly in the next chapter where we show how it goes to some lengths to identify and emphasize intergroup conflict in the new African states and laments the 'premature' departure of the white man. A foretaste of this is offered in Joubert's section on South African history in order to show the need for separate development (p. 247):

The neglect or failure to recognize the fact of ethnic nationalism was probably the biggest mistake revealed by recent African history north of the Limpopo. When peoples with divergent aspirations are thrown together, the smaller, weaker groups inevitably lose out. Conflict and strife follow. Separate development tries to take account of this. It therefore does not stop at segregation between White and Black, but also imposes segregation between one nation and another.

From this it would seem that nation and ethnicity are to be regarded as equivalent in the case of the blacks, but not in the case of the whites. Otherwise it would be logical to impose segregation between English- and Afrikaans-speaking whites as well.

The Joubert text's interpretation of separate development portrays the policy as progressive and largely unopposed. Dissent is dealt with in two main ways: first by omitting reference to it and, second, where it becomes absolutely necessary, by attributing it to external forces. Thus there is no mention of black political parties, such as the African National Congress (ANC) and the Pan African Congress (PAC), other than to note that they were banned by the South African Government. Nor are riots, school boycotts, defiance of pass laws and other evidence of opposition to the system dealt with. It is interesting that, while this textbook earlier devoted considerable attention to white intergroup conflict and implicitly condoned Afrikaner dissent, this is not the case with black opposition. No parallels have been drawn, for example, between the underdog role of the Afrikaner at the beginning of the century and the position of black people in South Africa. While it was legitimate for white Afrikaners to fight for their political rights, it is evidently not so for blacks.

The tendency is to attribute such opposition as is identified to external forces in both this and the Van Rensberg and Schoeman texts. The most common force identified is that of communist influence, which is frequently referred to in relation to labour disputes. Thus, for example, in Joubert: 'In August 1946 Black mineworkers, evidently incited by communist agitators went on strike; the strike had to be forcibly suppressed' (p. 189).

Another approach used in this book is to highlight what is perceived as the 'progressive' nature of separate development (p. 126):

Since 1948 the policy of apartheid has undergone a metamorphosis. Apartheid had many negative characteristics, but with Dr H. Verwoerd as the architect, it developed to become the more positive policy of Separate Development.

To give substance to this argument, the text then sets out to show what the government is doing to develop the so-called black states and how much 'progress' has been achieved.

The second textbook, by Boyce (1974*b*), adopts a quite different approach to Joubert. On the opening page of the chapter on separate development (p. 278) the reader is told:

The information which follows is an attempt to provide a completely factual account of the legislation of the Government since 1948. The writer of contemporary history is too close to the events of this period of history to have a sense of perspective because he lacks a knowledge of the significance of the events of the period—the historian is too close to know the results of events which have occurred in his time. Therefore the student of contemporary history should have an 'open mind' in approaching this field of studies; the questions asked are more important than the answers given.

In adopting this approach the account avoids falling into the trap of endorsing official ideology, but at the same time, by playing safe and sticking to facts, it does not in any way challenge the status quo.

There is no appeal to previous history to suggest that the practices of apartheid are sanctified by time, but an account is given of the legislation that supports it and of the underlying rationale. Rather than resorting to the rhetoric of national identity and separate nations more fundamental factors are said to be at work. For example: 'Fear of the consequences of Bantu urbanization as a result of economic integration undoubtedly affected the reasoning of South Africans on the subject of race relations' (p. 276).

It is also suggested that Afrikaner nationalism was used to provide a rationale for apartheid. In this respect the reader is told (via reference to another text) that 'as Afrikaner nationalism grew in the 1940s, the tendency to compromise disappeared and the apartheid idea came to the fore as the Afrikaners' uncompromising answer to the challenge of the native question' (Rhoodie and Venter, cited in Boyce, 1974b, p. 277).

The problems of classifying people by racial group are discussed. It is pointed out that classification revealed 'many tragic cases' that did not fit clearly into any category and that 'much humiliation, anxiety and resentment has resulted from official investigation into such cases' (Neame, 1962, in Boyce, 1974b, p. 278). Again this contrasts with the previous rosy picture of people pursuing their national identities in their separate communities.

The fundamental difference between this and the previous text is therefore that while this, albeit fairly uncritically, shows how the lives of black people have increasingly been subordinated to the controls imposed by white rule, Joubert's text attempts to show that, rather than being manipulated, the black groups are being allowed to pursue their own destinies in their own 'nations'. In common with Joubert, Boyce's textbook also underplays the role of conflict and dissent and disregards the role of black opposition. The interpretation therefore tends to represent the black groups as passive in the face of increasing subordination.

Perhaps because it has been written for the black education system, the Van Rensburg and Schoeman (1980b) textbook does give more attention to dissent. For example, the authors devote over two pages of their text to a description of the origin and aims of the African National Congress (ANC). However, it is noticeable that a clear distinction is made between black resistance before and after the introduction of the policy of separate development.

The early black political movements are accorded a degree of legitimacy in the text when, having noted the inferior status of black groups after the Union in 1910, it presents the ANC as an instrument for redressing this imbalance by constitutional means. By contrast, black resistance after 1948 is presented in a very different light. In common with Joubert, the Van Rensberg and Schoeman interpretation also attributes dissent to outside influences, particularly communist. For example, on page 229 the reader is told:

Since the National Party took over in 1948 there has been more or less chronic resistance to the White government on the part of Black activists supported by organizations such as the ANC. Later on the Pan Africanist Congress, in collaboration with Communist groups, also responded. As the government took action against resistance movements, so the nature of the opposition changed from passive resistance and civil disobedience to subversion and sabotage.

In detailing the various forms of opposition that have occurred since the implementation of apartheid, it is noticeable that the textbook makes little attempt to link this with the political and social status of black people in South Africa. The emphasis is instead put on 'political agitation' and 'intimidation' with black resistance presented as 'subversion'. Such an interpretation again contrasts sharply with these authors' perceptions of Afrikaner resistance to British influence.

In a less explicit way than in Joubert, the Van Rensburg and Schoeman text also shows a tendency to legitimate the status quo in South Africa. Because it is written for the black education system, this is partly disguised by the authors' attempt to give a black perspective. However, in reality this amounts to little more than window-dressing, and a white-centred approach, according with official policy, dominates the text.

This shows up in the introduction to the topic of 'Separate Development'. Here, rather than stressing the notion of white control and white interests, it presents apartheid as being of benefit to black people and following a natural course in history. Thus we learn on page 220:

> Gradually the idea took root that the Black reserves had to be developed into real national and political homes for Black people; that Blacks should for the most part live in these areas and that their influx into areas of White ownership should be limited; that in the reserves they should be given the opportunity to live and develop in their own way politically and in other ways. These ideas culminated in the policy of Separate Development: a policy of multi-nationality.

The tendency to present apartheid as a natural historical development is also evident when the readers are told that it is based on 'the traditional principles of separation'. It is traditional, according to the text, because 'the idea of segregation can be traced back to the first encounters between Black and White on the eastern frontier of the Cape Colony' (p. 225). However, because there is no explanation of how and why such segregation arose, it is made to appear as de facto natural.

The section on separate development closes on an optimistic note, stressing the prospect of racial harmony (p. 231):

> By the end of 1979 there was ample sign of a change of heart in South Africa. The government had departed from their strict implementation of discriminatory measures based on colour alone.... Indeed, the outlook for racial peace and prosperity and a common, binding South African nationalism and patriotism has never been better.

THE INDIANS

All three textbooks represent the Indian group as a 'problem'; though they differ in the way this problem is perceived. The distinction is most clear in the Boyce (1974*b*) and Joubert (1979) texts and we will concentrate on these.

Joubert's view of the Indians as a problem is explicit from the start, as the opening paragraph reveals (p. 258):

> In Standard Nine we learnt that the Indians were first brought to Natal in 1860. As the years passed, they began to create certain problems. By the time of Union in 1910, they had become a national problem. Several repatriation schemes after this date also came to nothing, because after this date there were too many Indians (30,000) who had been born in South Africa and refused to leave.

As with its presentation of the black 'problem', the Joubert text makes no attempt to tell his reader what the Indian problem is and initially it seems that this must, in some way, relate to their numerical status. It is only after discussion of the various attempts made by governments to enforce repatriation that the reader finally has a clue as to what this problem is all about. In the meantime, the Indian pupil who reads the text, far from learning something about his or her ancestors' contribution to South African history, learns only that they were a 'problem' and needed to be 'repatriated'. To add to this indignity, the Indian pupil also learns that his forbears' religious and social attitudes 'went against the Christian principles of the Whites' and that 'most of the Indians were descended from the lowest castes in India' (p. 259).

The 'problem', it eventually transpires, concerns Indian participation in South Africa's retail sector. It appears that Indian success in this area of the economy was greatly resented by white traders, who lobbied fiercely to restrict their activities. It is the manner in which the Joubert text deals with the matter which betrays its white-centred approach. For example, the word 'encroach' is used to describe Indian expansion in retail trade, rather than, say, 'compete', thereby suggesting that the Indians were acting unfairly or even illegally by competing with white traders. An alternative interpretation that might have been offered from a less exclusively white point of view is that Indian traders made a contribution to the development of the retail sector.

Boyce's textbook does make an effort in this direction, and it stresses the contribution made by the Indians to South Africa's economic development: 'The sugar industry flourished as a result of the Indian labourers, and later as free men they contributed a great deal to the economic development of the colony [Natal]' (p. 293). While Boyce also uses the term 'Indian problem', there is an attempt to show that this is how it was perceived by white traders of the time, without diminishing the Indian contribution: 'As the Indian population multiplied and spread over the colony [Natal], the Whites took fright and became antagonistic towards those Indians who displayed initiative and enterprise in trading and farming' (p. 293).

This textbook, however, is also prone to some unfortunate turns of phrase. In particular a number of references are made to the 'penetration' and 'infiltration' by Indians into white residential areas, leaving the impression that somehow they had no business being there.

Finally, all three authors show a tendency to stress the increase in the Indian birth-rate as a problem in itself, whereas the high birth-rate among rural Afrikaners and the increase of the white population generally is never commented on in this way.

THE COLOUREDS

Like the Indians, the coloureds are dealt with from an essentially white point of view. Only Boyce offers a brief summary of coloured history. Otherwise the texts concentrate on the legislation defining their political status and their role in the economy.

Until 1956, coloured people living in Cape Province held the same franchise as whites in South Africa. After that date they were effectively disenfranchised when they were removed from the common voters' roll and placed on a separate one which entitled them to white representation in the House of Assembly (parliament). Their political rights were further eroded in 1968 when they lost this parliamentary representation. This was replaced by an autonomous body, the Coloured People's Representative Council (CPRC),[1] which was created to advise government on matters relating to coloured people. The CPRC was partly elected by the community it was intended to serve and partly nominated by government itself. Rather than describing this process as an erosion of political rights, the texts tend to present it as political progress following a natural and inevitable course. Most explicit in this respect is Joubert (1979, p. 274):

1. The CPRC was abolished in April 1980 and replaced by the Coloured Persons' Council.

Meanwhile (since 1959) the idea that the Coloureds should manage their own affairs had taken root, and in 1964 the necessary legislation for a Coloured People's Representative Council was prepared. The Coloureds' White representatives now became unnecessary.

Van Rensburg and Schoeman's textbook stresses the need to change the coloured franchise in the interests of 'uniformity', for prior to 1956 there was no coloured franchise in the Orange Free State and Natal.

Another consideration put forward in support of the new arrangements is the suggestion that the coloured vote did not have much significance in the first place, so that disenfranchisement was not really as regressive as critics might claim. For example, all authors make the point that when the franchise was extended to white women in 1931, the influence of the coloured vote declined. The validity of this claim is however in some doubt, as De Villiers indicates that the coloured vote could in fact exercise a decisive influence on the outcome of an election (in ten of the fifty-eight Cape constituencies), even though white women were given the franchise (De Villiers, 1979, p. 43).

Finally, we come to the textbooks' treatment of the role of the coloured people in the South African economy. The most significant feature here is that little attempt is made to elaborate on the legislation and other factors that have determined this group's disadvantaged position in the class structure, which instead is made to appear a 'natural' one in a fixed social order. In Van Rensburg and Schoeman we are told that coloureds mostly work as agricultural labourers and domestic servants in rural areas, and as factory workers and bricklayers in the urban sector. In Joubert, we are even informed that 'there are some trades like joinery and bricklaying for which the Coloured seems to have a natural aptitude, and in which he performs exceptionally well' (p. 271). Nowhere in these discussions is there any reference to such factors as job reservation, differential salaries for white and coloured workers, or the exclusion of coloureds from 'open' universities, which might go some way towards explaining why members of this group occupy the kind of positions they do.

Having stressed the coloureds' position mainly at the lower end of the social structure, the texts then go on to show that this group is, none the less, upwardly mobile and the reader is presented with facts and figures to show that 'progress' is being made. Joubert's text notes that at a professional level 'the Coloured has still to make up a lot of leeway' (p. 271). Again the suggestion is that this leeway results from a failure on the part of the 'the Coloured' rather than from structural constraints.

Summary

It is evident that the contemporary history syllabus around which the textbooks have been written is intended to reflect 'separate development' as the norm among South Africa's population groups. The history of white groups is given prominence until the formal introduction of the policy of apartheid, at which point non-white groups become the focus of attention. We have pointed out that these syllabus divisions are artificial but that the intention has been to present different groups as having separate histories and destinies. This accords explicitly with the ideology of apartheid.

We have also noted that even where a section on non-white history is specified in the syllabus, this is presented in the textbooks entirely from a white perspective. In this respect, the history of blacks, coloureds and Indians is merely an account of white-imposed legislation that has determined the role of non-whites in the polity and economy of South Africa.

A further finding in this section of the analysis is that in two of the three textbooks attempts have been made to present South Africa's social structure (based on a racial division of labour) as a 'natural order' with historical antecedents. This has been done by ignoring the structural and legal factors which in reality have combined to create a highly inegalitarian society.

Finally, a general pattern which emerges from this examination of textbooks is that while legitimation is implicitly accorded to forms of dissent among white groups, this is not the case with non-whites. Forms of black opposition to white supremacy are, in this respect, either ignored or ascribed to external forces such as communism rather than to the prevailing circumstances of inequality.

7 Social and political change in Africa

Introduction

In this chapter we examine how the textbooks view the outside world, or at least that part of it with most apparent relevance to the situation in South Africa. The books are the same as those reviewed in the previous chapter, the Standard 10 texts by Joubert (1979), Boyce (1974*b*), and Van Rensburg and Schoeman (1980*b*), and the section of the syllabus considered is that entitled 'New Africa North of the Zambezi'.

Once again we pay particular attention to the way conflict is handled. We have also sought to examine how far parallels are drawn between the processes of historical change in Black Africa and in South Africa itself. For in this connection the authors are faced with the problem of reconciling white domination at home with black majority rule elsewhere in Africa. Decolonization has been going on since the 1950s and the recent independence of South Africa's immediate neighbours, Angola, Mozambique and Zimbabwe, has brought the spectre of black majority rule right to South Africa's borders. At the same time, her own racial policies have come increasingly under attack from the African continent, other world governments and the United Nations.

We have, therefore, attempted in our analysis, to see how the textbooks have dealt with this contradiction; whether, for example, they link decolonization in Africa with the establishment of so called black states in South Africa, or whether perhaps the consequences of decolonization are used as justification for apartheid. As we shall see the authors employ a number of different strategies.

Table 22 shows the topics specified by the Black African section of the syllabus and the proportion of space allocated in the three textbooks.

Boyce's textbook devotes much more space to this section than the other two, paying particular attention to 'Independence Movements and Nationalism'. In this way this text gives a much broader historical background than the others. Surprisingly, perhaps, the Van Rensburg text written for blacks gives the topic least space.

The fact that the syllabus specifies a topic on 'Problems in African States' helps to predefine the approach adopted, in that authors are asked to attend to the things that have gone wrong in the new states. The inclusion of a topic on

'China's Interest in Africa' shows the syllabus writer's preoccupation with communism.

TABLE 22. 'New Africa North of the Zambezi' (Section 5 of Standard 10 general history): percentages of total general history

Syllabus topic	Boyce	Joubert	Van Rensburg
Post-war independence movements and the impact of nationalism in Africa as an introduction	24.5	4.0	8.0
The common problems faced by the independent African states—political, economic, social	3.6	4.2	4.0
The Third World and the Organization of African Unity	0.7	6.0	4.8
China's interest in Africa	1.4	6.4	
Percentage of total general history	30.2	20.6	17.4[1]

1. Includes additional material in the text.

Political change

All three texts trace the rise of nationalism and independence movements on the continent. This is followed by an examination of common problems faced by the new states.

Although the three textbooks approach the subject somewhat differently, they also share a certain amount of common ground. In particular, all implicitly see a failure to conform to Western-style democracy as a key problem in African political development. Thus deviations from this model are stressed, such as coups, military takeovers, and the rise of the one-party state.

The most ethnocentric interpretation is in Joubert's text, which lacks the kind of historical perspective that would be provided by a serious consideration of the impact of colonial rule on subsequent political structures. Thus political and administrative problems are presented as inherent in African societies themselves and defined largely in terms of failure to adapt to democracy and the departure of the white men after independence. In addition, Joubert's textbook shows a strong tendency to generalize, so that political change in Africa appears as a uniform process of upheaval across the continent. From such generalizations emerge explicit stereotypes. For example, on page 132:

Bribery, speculation and rank inexperience brought many states to the verge of chaos. State finances were a major headache in most countries where ignorance led to corruption and wastage, as in Ghana, which in turn led more than once to bankruptcy.

Political coups and one-party states are other aspects of the failure of democracy: 'the political coups of later years and the rise of the one-party system of government indicate that Western democracy had not entrenched itself very deeply in the African mind' (p. 127). Ethnic divisions are part of the reason for this (p. 133):

Opposition parties often tended to be ethnic opposition groups who, instead of pursuing policies of constructive criticism, as one would expect from a genuine parliamentary opposition, aimed rather at destroying the government, assuming power and pursuing their own ethnic interests.

Implicitly South Africa's system of dealing with ethnic divisions is to be preferred.

Another striking dimension of Joubert's account is its tendency to define political problems in terms of the departure of the white man following African independence. The problem as such is termed 'localization' (the process of replacing white administrators with local citizens). Implicit in this is the idea that Africans are unready to take over leadership and administration of their countries without the help of the white man (p. 152):

Some of the Whites left of their own accord but quite a number were simply forced to quit. The Africans who succeeded the Whites seldom had any experience of the jobs they now had to fill, resulting in serious problems. As a result, standards in the public services dropped alarmingly.

By way of contrast, we are then presented (p. 133) with the example of one African leader, Félix Houphouët-Boigny of the Ivory Coast, who defied the general trend:

Houphouët Boigny, realized the need for retaining White officials for many years after independence, if administrative chaos was to be avoided.... The Ivory Coast remains one of the few African states with a healthy trade balance.

This example illustrates another tendency in Joubert's approach. While the overall interpretation tends towards generalization, a few extreme examples are used to add weight to the argument, giving a highly unbalanced picture polarized towards one point of view. Along with the lack of background on the impact of colonialism, this means that the reader is given little opportunity to draw his or her own conclusions from the text.

By comparison, Boyce's textbook is more balanced, and attempts to present different points of view. In particular the book sets the analysis in a historical perspective, which allows a much better understanding of contemporary change in Africa. Thus, by examining the impact of colonial rule on African societies the text does not suggest that subsequent problems in political development are inherent in the countries or people themselves, but rather the outcome of dislocation resulting from the imposition of one political system on others.

This textbook is also less prone than the previous one to indulge in broad generalizations, but attempts to differentiate the experiences of individual countries. Following from this, what are perceived as common problems are drawn out at the conclusion of the analysis. The overwhelming portion of the text is devoted to a detailed analysis of the rise of independence movements and nationalism, and their antecedents in colonial rule, with only a very small proportion devoted to common problems. For example, in citing political instability as the major problem facing post-independent African governments, this textbook shows how colonial rule created national boundaries where there had never been any real unity in the past, and that the problem is one of trying to forge a national identity in the face of conflicting ethnic and regional interests.

It is considerations such as these which make this textbook's treatment of conflict more sympathetic than Joubert's and enables the rise of the one-party state in Africa to be presented as a response to the prevailing conditions, rather than as a political aberration (p. 196):

Many African leaders claimed that the creation of a 'one-party state' was essential for the welfare of the nation. These single parties constructed the most effective organizational networks before independence and the African governments have used this network to secure wide national support.

While Boyce's textbook does not explicitly condone the one-party state (it is the African leaders who defend it), it does acknowledge that the mass party has the potential to fulfil a number of integrative functions. For example (p. 196):

In nations where the party is an effective and real one regular meetings take place. These meetings are the means whereby the government... transmits new ideas, new projects, etc., to the people. They thus educate the population and in this way enlist its energies in the service of the nation.

This approach allows the one-party system to be seen as a step towards the same kind of democratic ideal that is implicit in the Joubert text (Boyce, p. 196):

There is thus a correlation between the strength of the party and leader and the degree of national integration and stability. It is this integration and stability that make possible economic development and increase the ultimate prospects for a flexible democracy in Africa.

The Boyce text also cites 'localization' as a problem facing independent African states. However, unlike Joubert's interpretation, which presents the problem solely in terms of a white exodus, it makes some attempt to look at underlying causes and stresses the failure of colonial rule to create the necessary infrastructure (p. 195):

The administrative services inherited from the colonial governments had two major weaknesses. Firstly, the senior personnel of the colonial administration came from the metropolitan or mother countries. When they withdrew on independence, their posts were filled by Africans who had no suitable or adequate training for them. Secondly, the colonial administration was limited in character. Colonial governments had been primarily interested in upholding law and order and creating satisfactory conditions for trade and investment.

Our third textbook, by Van Rensburg and Schoeman, falls somewhere between Joubert and Boyce in its interpretation of political change in Africa. It remains ethnocentric but makes some attempt to provide an appropriate historical context and to differentiate between various countries' experiences. Since the text is written specifically for the black education system the authors face the obvious problem of how far their readers should be encouraged to identify with Black Africa as a whole. It appears that this is thought acceptable providing that their political aspirations take the form of a desire for a homeland under the apartheid system (p. 113):

The concept of a people sharing common values and common identity can also relate to the ethnic group. When groups such as the Bakongo (Zaire), the Tswana (Bophuthatswana) or the Oxhosa (Transkei) ask for separate political status they are expressing what may be called ethnic nationalism.

How far South Africans in the Transkei and elsewhere have 'asked' for 'separate political status' is a question that is not pursued. We saw a similar attempt in Van Rensburg et al.'s (1976) Standard 8 text to equate a sense of ethnic identity with black support for separate development. However, the overwhelming tendency is to treat development in Black Africa as a quite distinct process—something that is happening 'out there' and, implicitly, that cannot be identified within South African terms.

Van Rensburg and Schoeman's interpretation acknowledges the impact of colonial rule on post-independence political problems, since this is difficult to ignore, but the consequences of colonialism are played down (p. 122):

Yet while it is beyond question that many of the problems now facing African nations can be traced back to the colonial period, it is equally true that many of the root causes lie much further back in pre-colonial African societies and cultures.

It is even suggested, on page 122, that preoccupation with colonialism is part of the present problems:

The colonial period, with all its benefits or ills, is now a fact of history. Independent African governments have accepted the fact that they must work within the old colonial boundaries and that they must face the realities of the day. Nevertheless, many intellectuals in Africa are still pre-occupied with the colonial past, and this fact, with all its psychological implications, is fundamental to any understanding of the present problems of our continent.

This line of argument, which appears elsewhere in this text, might be thought to be an attempt to discourage black students from inquiring too closely into the colonial phase of African history.

The 'failure of parliamentary democracy' is said to be a major problem in the new states, though the reasons for the failure are little explored; but attention is drawn to its consequences in the by-now-familiar inventory of dictatorships, one-party systems and military takeovers. To emphasize the point the case of Ghana is then presented (p. 123):

An outstanding example is Ghana. Nkrumah had become increasingly high-handed and silenced all open opposition but failed to prevent the corruption of his own supporters. He followed strongly anti-Western foreign policies which lost him support of Western businessmen and governments—which, in turn, worsened his already struggling economy. The result in 1965 was a coup, strongly approved by Western interests. The army declared that their intention was to purify the administration and follow more realistic economic and foreign policies.

While appearing to be somewhat ambivalent towards the idea of one-party systems, the text (p. 123) acknowledges that

the new African states, because of their level of political development, their economic and social position, and the accompanying problems of nation-building, need strong leadership. Because Western institutions do not always provide this, the one-party system is probably the best under existing circumstances. A responsible dictator is sometimes preferable to political corruption.

Another political problem identified in Van Rensburg and Schoeman is that of 'tribalism' and 'tribal separation'. The text recognizes the role of colonial rule in creating boundaries that transcended ethnic divisions, thus creating an obstacle to nation-building, and acknowledges that the colonial authorities 'often found that it was in their own interests to play one tribal group off against another'.

Finally Van Rensburg and Schoeman cite localization as a problem, with white officials being replaced by untrained blacks. The treatment of this matter is punctuated by a curious reference to the case of Angola where 'President Neto replaced Whites by Cubans who added another problem to the existing troubles of Angola' (p. 124). Cubans are clearly thought to be a particularly undesirable type of non-white!

Social and economic problems

In discussing the social and economic problems facing the new African nations, all textbooks implicitly present the African states as 'backward' and in need of 'modernization'. It is taken for granted that modernization should follow the Western industrial model.

Once again it is in Joubert that we find the most explicitly ethnocentric interpretation. Much weight is placed on the 'untimely' departure of the white man from the continent, the idea that independence came too early (p. 134):

The economy of the African territories, like their administration, used to be in the hands of the colonial powers and to rely on White initiative. Notwithstanding the emergent African's firm belief, colonisation did not imply exploitation only. The Whites contributed considerably to the economic development of the continent. Independence thus also brought economic problems for the African states.

We are told on pages 134–5 that, despite the availability of outside capital for development,

using the capital to the best advantage proved to be even a greater problem than acquiring it because once again, the African's lack of experience proved to be a major stumbling block. Development was held up by the building of multi-million prestige projects rather than essential but less prestigious projects and services.... Only time can provide the African states with the experience needed to cope with economic problems. Large-scale development projects are at present being undertaken by overseas companies with the assistance of their own technicians.

Joubert's textbook tends to ascribe economic failure to an inherent state of 'backwardness' in the African countries themselves. To demonstrate this, figures are given to show Africa's dependence on agriculture as compared with Western Europe and America. To add weight to his argument, we are then shown how dependent African countries are on foreign aid and expertise (a photograph amplifying this point is printed in the text showing a white agriculture officer 'providing guidance to a Kenyan farmer'). The untimely-departure thesis is also used to explain technological and educational backwardness.

Boyce's treatment is more comprehensive than Joubert's. The interpretation of contemporary economic and social problems is set within the framework of colonial dependency. However, the basic premise is that development must occur from within Africa, and so the text pays little attention to external factors such as the control of prices for primary commodities, which may retard economic development.

This section of the book begins by setting the topic in the context of colonial economic dependency (p. 196):

> From the outset of independence African leaders have asserted almost unanimously that the political advantage gained through the struggle for independence will be rendered meaningless without a corresponding advance in economic independence.

It shows how, under colonial rule, economic power was in the hands of the metropolitan countries and that the colonies operated to produce raw materials for the mother country, while manufactured goods were imported.

We are then informed (p. 196):

> Economically the new states were bound hand and foot and they realized that if their political independence was to be given any economic substance, they had to develop their economies in the light of their own needs, their relationship to their African neighbours and their relationship to the rest of the world. This is the reality of independence which the Africans now seek.

Having established the fact that economic decolonization is a necessary precondition for economic development and the raising of living standards, the text then goes on to present what is seen as the solution. This, we learn, is a threefold task: first, the creation of a balanced economy suited to the conditions of each state: second, the development of industry and exploitation of natural resources; and third, the modernization of agriculture and transformation of rural life.

This prescription implies a particular model of development, based on the Western capitalist experience. The problem becomes defined in terms of how to 'catch up' or how to 'modernize'. Implicitly, obstacles to economic development are perceived as inherent in the African countries themselves and the old clichés of 'backwardness' and 'lack of experience and knowledge' are invoked. It should perhaps be mentioned here that this approach is not peculiar to Boyce, but has permeated orthodox development thinking since the early days of decolonization. This approach has increasingly been challenged as development strategies based on it have failed to bear fruit. More and more development theorists have begun to question whether it is possible or even desirable for poor countries to develop on the model of the industrial democracies. It has become clear that many of the causes of underdevelopment lie in the international political and economic order and not just in the social and economic arrangements in the poor countries themselves. Some have argued that the existing pattern of links with the developed world is the main obstacle to meaningful development in the Third World and that a new international economic order is a prerequisite of any significant reduction in poverty-generating dependency in developing countries. This type of approach to the problems of development is not explored in any of the textbooks.

We learn from Boyce's text that the 'economic backwardness' of the African countries stands in the way of adequate capital formation; that without adequate scientific and technical skills the development of modern industry will 'lag behind'; that incentives must be given to persuade the conservative peasant to change his 'age-old' farming methods; and that education is needed if the African states are to keep pace in the 'race for modernization'.

This same approach permeates Boyce's treatment of social problems facing the new African countries, where we are told (p. 198): 'One of the major problems which all the states which have recently achieved their independence have to face is the reorganization of their social structure to conform to the new political, economic and moral ideas of modern life.' The phrase 'reorganization of their social structure' merely signifies the need for education, improved health care and checks on urbanization. Education is needed because it creates the base upon which the 'functioning of democratic institutions is possible'.

This textbook, none the less, does treat the topic a good deal more comprehensively than either of the other two, with more attention to detail and explanation. Moreover, the interpretations offered are not as prone to ethnocentricity.

The third textbook, by Van Rensburg and Schoeman, treats economic and social problems in considerably less detail than Boyce. The overall picture presented is a highly generalized and simplistic one, with little attempt to differentiate between countries, or to examine underlying causes. Indeed, what we are given is really only a list of unqualified facts and figures.

For example, under the first economic problem, entitled 'Limited Economic Sovereignty', we learn (p. 124):

With independence the African states achieved political independence. But they were not viable economic units. Their economic dependence on their former colonial overlords made them nothing more than 'mini states'. Let us look at some statistics: Black Africa contains almost 400 million or people 8 per cent of the world's population. Yet it produces only 1 per cent of the world's Gross National Product (GNP). The income per head only increases at a rate of 1.5 per cent annually.

Africa therefore is dependent on economic aid from outside and this, in turn, affects its political independence.

Here we can see the ambiguity which characterizes the Van Rensburg and Schoeman interpretation. In essence, what the text appears to be suggesting is that African states are dependent on aid because they are not viable economic units and their GNP is so low. The reference to their dependence on their colonial overlords making them nothing more than 'mini' states does little to explain the problem as originally stated, namely limited economic sovereignty. Whereas in Boyce the problem is described in terms of dependent economies with strong ties to the metropolitan countries, in Van Rensburg and Schoeman the problem is twisted round: that is, because they are so poor they are dependent. In this way, the colonial impact on subsequent economic development is minimized. Moreover, continuing economic dependency through links with the international economy is entirely neglected, except in passing reference in the second stated problem, the colonial heritage. Here we at least are informed of the origins of single-product economies and their vulnerability to world prices.

Obstacles to foreign investment figure fairly prominently in this textbook's interpretation of economic problems. We are told that Western investors have been unwilling to put money into unstable countries or those where foreign-owned enterprises are likely to be nationalized. The fact that African leaders resent foreign companies making profits out of African resources is also pointed out.

'Socialism' is also cited as an economic problem (p. 124):

Independent Africa has accepted African Socialism as its economic ideology. Blacks in Africa have adopted this because it suits the natural communal character of the African people, because European socialists were the enemies of colonialism and because socialism offered the best chance of development of underdeveloped countries.

Having acknowledged that socialism may be appropriate to the African context, the text then rejects it as being economically unviable, giving the United Republic of Tanzania as an example (p. 125):

In Tanzania this [socialism] has killed the initiative of smallholders with the result that Tanzania which in the colonial period produced enough food, nowadays has to import foodstuffs to the value of R300 million annually. Nationalization has also frightened foreign investors.

The remedy for Africa's economic ills as prescribed in Van Rensburg and Schoeman is 'large-scale investment in agriculture and the development of simple diversified industries which can produce manufactured goods for the home market'. But again it is a problem of attracting foreign investment. Like the other two textbooks the Van Rensburg and Schoeman book subscribes to the 'modernization/catching up' theory of development.

African unity

The Standard 10 general syllabus section 'New Africa North of the Zambesi' specifies as a topic 'The Organization of African Unity' (OAU). The OAU was founded in 1963 and was the outcome of a number of earlier attempts to forge some form of unity among the newly independent African countries. Its origins lie in the philosophy of Pan-Africanism espoused by some of the leaders of the early independence movements, most notably Kwame Nkrumah of Ghana. The original idea of unity was thus derived from the common experience of colonialism, and as Oliver and Fage (1970) have pointed out, was 'further cemented by their community of opposition to the continuing presence of White domination in the South of the continent' (p. 267).

Among the aims of the OAU are the promotion of unity and solidarity among African states; the co-ordination of efforts to improve living standards on the continent; the defence of sovereignty, territorial integrity and independence; the eradication of all forms of colonialism in Africa; and the promotion of international co-operation. Since the ideas behind the OAU are in direct conflict with the maintenance of the status quo in South Africa, the organization is seen as a 'threat' to that country.

The fact that two of the three textbooks (by Joubert, and Van Rensburg and Schoeman) devote more space to this topic than to common problems in Africa is some indication of the importance which they attach to it. There is, however, a distinct ambivalence in their treatment of the OAU. On the one hand the 'threat' aspect is stressed, for example, by reference to the OAU's aid to liberation movements in southern Africa. On the other hand there is a tendency to emphasize the problems and weaknesses of the OAU, which helps to minimize the perceived threat. In this there is in some cases more than a hint of the familiar white assumption of African incompetence. But then, if the OAU is as incompetent and divided as is made out, the reader begins to wonder why it warrants so much attention.

Joubert's textbook shows this ambivalence in an early paragraph (pp. 140–1).

An important factor uniting the member countries of the OAU is the common antagonism towards the White people of Southern Africa. In certain respects the establishment of the OAU was yet another attempt to end white rule in Southern Africa. But there are problems within the OAU itself, problems that impair the unity of the body.

One of the problems mentioned is 'territorial and ethnic disputes', which, we are told, 'tend to tarnish the image of African unity'. Another problem is 'jealousies amongst the states'. To illustrate this the text explains that when the Secretariat was set up in 1963 so many leaders aspired to the post of Secretary-General that four assistant-secretaries eventually had to be appointed as well. This is followed, on page 143, by an extraordinary and misleading account of confrontation between African leaders:

During the second Summit, Nyerere attacked Nkrumah while thousands were watching the proceedings on television. Nkrumah, in turn, ridiculed the Liberation Front, with its headquarters in Dar-es-Salaam. During the third Summit Meeting no fewer than eight African states attacked Nkrumah for having given refuge to fugitives from their countries.

The 'attacks', it turns out, were purely verbal. This clearly seeks to make the most of signs of disunity in the organization, and so what is being presented as aggressive behaviour, is in fact what takes place in every forum where decisions are taken on the basis of representation and debate, even in Cape Town's Houses of Parliament.

The third heading in Joubert's list of OAU problems is 'the African Liberation Committee and its Problems'. The African Liberation Committee represents the most direct threat to South Africa. Its main problem according to this textbook is that it does not have enough money to do its work properly. Not only is it underfunded, but 'in addition, a good deal of this money was squandered by Committee members on such luxuries as motor cars, parties and luxurious mansions' (p. 143).

Thus the members are represented as irresponsible and uncommitted. So much so, it seems, that subsequently even the Soviet Union and China withdrew their aid to this committee when the liberation campaign (unspecified) failed to materialize. Furthermore, we are told that the African Liberation Committee has been unable to reconcile the splits between various competing 'terrorist organizations'. Here mention is made of the Angolan liberation movements and the Rhodesian ones. It is significant that nowhere in the section devoted to this committee is there any reference to the South African liberation movements, the African National Congress, Pan-African Congress, or South West African People's Organization. The section on the African Liberation Committee concludes with the acknowledgement that 'the successes achieved by terrorist organizations in territories such as Angola and Mozambique, can to a large extent be attributed to physical and moral support received from amongst others the OAU' (p. 143). It then goes on to point out that, despite its problems, the OAU has acted as a unified body in its relations with the rest of the world, has maintained an independent identity in the so-called communist–democracy confrontation on the continent, and has combined with the Asian countries to form the largest power bloc in the United Nations, where they are able to launch attacks on the Republic.

Finally the section concludes: 'In spite of the unremitting anti-South African militancy of the OAU, South Africa has continued with her policy of dialogue in order to persuade the rest of Africa that Black and White can share this continent in peace' (p. 146).

The textbook by Boyce shows a tendency to stand back somewhat from politically contentious subject-matter in contemporary history, as we saw in its treatment of separate development in the previous chapter. Its approach is similar when dealing with the Organization of African Unity. The text is brief (350 words) and factual. It gives an account of the aims and origins of the OAU, making clear its commitment to the liberation of the southern part of the continent. References are even made to 'freedom fighters' (compared with the use of 'terrorist' in Joubert), and the 1972 United Nations resolution condemning all countries supplying arms to South Africa and appealing for trade boycotts, due to South Africa's 'occupation of Namibia'.

Here the text ends, and the students are presented with an exercise, which reads as follows (p. 202):

The following report entitled 'Ten Years of Turmoil' reprinted from *To the Point* (19 May 1973) states that the dream of African unity is no nearer reality than it was at the first meeting of the OAU ten years ago. What has the OAU achieved in the ten years (1963–73)?

This question is then followed by the report itself, which occupies as much space as the actual text (though in smaller print). The article in question is entirely negative in its treatment, as the title 'Ten Years of Turmoil' might suggest. Presumably the intention behind the exercise is to make the student think and draw his own conclusions. But since no alternative point of view is given, the student is being asked to make an evaluation on the basis of one extremely biased account. It should be noted that *To the Point* is a fortnightly magazine that was secretly funded by the South African Department of Information as a propaganda vehicle.

The report itself treats the topic in both a superficial and trivial way. It starts out by stating that the dream of African unity espoused by Haile Selassie and Kwame Nkrumah is no nearer reality than it was when it started. To emphasize the point this is immediately followed (p. 202) by a crude example:

There was even dissension over the body of Kwame Nkrumah who died last year far away from his continent. He had been forced to leave his homeland and died in a hospital in Rumania. After his death there was a macabre period of weeks during which Ghana and Guinea squabbled over his body. Finally the 'Redeemer' was laid to rest in his own country of Ghana.

There then follows example after example of what are presented as feuds, squabbles and power struggles among members. Much issue is made of the Libyan Arab Jamahiriya's attempt to put pressure on the OAU to adopt an anti-Israeli position, and we are given an alleged quote from an anonymous African journalist (he does not want his name disclosed because he fears for his life) which reads: 'The OAU was created to gain freedom for black Africa, but today it is being used by white Russians, yellow Chinese and brown Arabs to further their own interests, and in the process, to undermine the black man's independence' (p. 202).

The article goes on to say (pp. 202–3) that at a forthcoming meeting in Addis Ababa:

It is almost certain that the question of dialogue will be discussed once again; so will the problems of the liberation movements come under scrutiny and all the other contradictions that 'in reality reinforce the chaotic absurdity of mini-sovereignties as the plague of the continent', as one observer put it, while unity is preached only in the talking shop that is the OAU. Indeed it has become a feature of the OAU that it has made little social or technical impact.

And so the list of failures, conflicts and breaches reads on. It is difficult to see how, in the absence of any alternative interpretation, the student can avoid arriving at a negative evaluation of the OAU. Boyce's treatment of the topic would hardly seem to accord with the aim of the syllabus 'To educate to an objective approach towards history, fostering the habit of first investigating all relevant facts before passing judgement' (Item 3.9, Appendix 5).

Over half the Van Rensburg and Schoeman text is taken up in presenting the origins, aims and functions of the OAU; the rest discusses its problems and achievements. The text shows the same kind of ambivalence that we noted in Joubert, heightened by an awareness of the likely sensibilities of its black readership. The section opens on a sympathetic note (p. 127):

African nationalism is like a great forest tree. Its trunk is the Pan-African movement, which gives a sense of solidarity to all the different people of the continent. Its branches are the independent states of Africa. As the roots of the tree reach deep into the soil, so the origins of African nationalism spread in many directions back into history.

The authors then trace the origins of African nationalism from the days of slavery. They note that Marcus Garvey, Jamaican founder of the 'Back to Africa' movement, was 'as racially exclusive as the White settlers in colonial Africa' (p. 127). Perhaps it would be reading too much into the text to see this as an oblique attempt to co-opt elements of black nationalism to the cause of separate development, but that is a tendency that we have noted in this text before.

The textbook's discussion of OAU problems echoes its account of the problems of the new African states. Political problems centre around the question of nation-building; the continent is inhabited by a variety of peoples 'ranging from Arabs and Negroes to Asians, Coloureds, Europeans and Bushmen'. There are also ethnic minorities caught between national boundaries which have caused 'internal unrest'. In the same brief paragraph we are then told 'if the Africans cannot co-operate within a specified state, how can they ever hope to achieve continental unity?' (p. 130). Once again the ideal of separate development lurks in the background. The tendency is to suggest that racial integration does not work. Even the Arabs are grist to this mill: 'In the second place there is distrust between Black people and the Arabs as a result of the former Arab slave trade and because the Arabs are trying to promote the ideal of Pan-Arabism rather than Pan-Africanism' (p. 130).

On economic problems, in one short paragraph the authors repeat that because they are poor, African countries need external aid which they all compete for: 'Thus, instead of presenting a unified front in their dealing with the richer states, they are glorified beggar-states, only able to manage a bluff at unity now and again when they know that their individual patrons will not object' (p. 130).

The text then goes on to consider whether the OAU has been a success or a failure. First the successes. We are informed that despite its many glaring weaknesses and problems 'it is undeniably a wonderful organization', and that 'the OAU may lack teeth and bite, but it serves as the recognized platform for emergent Africa' (p. 131). Among its successes are its size as the biggest power bloc within the United Nations, where it has been able to assert itself on, among other things, decisions relating to racial discrimination in South Africa. Then there is the list of six disputes that it mediated in successfully, its success in bargaining with the European Common Market for favourable trade terms, and the establishment of the African Development Bank.

'Unfortunately,' it goes on, 'this list of the OAU's achievements is much shorter than that of its failings.' Then comes the list. At the top is the fact that almost every African state today is in economic difficulties. It is suggested that the reason economic problems have been unresolved by the OAU is because it has been more concerned with political issues, because 'these are usually more compelling and spectacular while economic difficulties develop subtly and are seldom so specific and dramatic'. The text also notes that 'Africans often console themselves by blaming the colonial past—and do very little about it' (p. 132), echoing the view expressed in its section on African political problems.

Another failure cited is that the OAU has been ineffectual in solving interstate conflict (in spite of the successful resolutions acknowledged earlier in the text) (p. 132):

The result of this situation is that some African countries have used their scarce money to buy arms for mutual destruction, instead of strengthening unity and by focusing attention on the priority areas of social and economic development.

In common with Joubert, the Van Rensburg and Schoeman book also taunts the OAU for failing to attain its goal of liberation on the African continent. Curiously African states are chided because 'the wars in Rhodesia and against South West Africa were financed and directed not by the OAU but by the Communists. And this had brought a bigger danger than ever before, in that Africa could lose its hard-won independence to Russian neo-colonialism' (p. 132). By a strange twist of logic the OAU, by failing to be as much of a threat to South Africa as it would like to be, is accused of introducing an even worse threat—communism.

It is made clear, however, that the OAU is not entirely toothless in its own right since it has been largely responsible for ending South Africa's participation in the Olympic Games and curtailing the supply of overseas military equipment to South Africa.

The section concludes on the same positive note on which it began: 'But when all is said and done, the OAU is in a sense an affirmation by Black Africans that they have an identity and ought to be listened to after centuries of being ignored' (p. 133). In the context of this book as a whole it is obvious that the inference that is meant to be drawn from this is that the best way of fostering black identity and listening to black voices is not the OAU way but the South African way.

Communism in Africa

The final topic in the section 'New Africa North on the Zambesi' is entitled 'China's Interest in Africa'. It is covered by only two of the three textbooks we have been considering, Joubert and Boyce, with the former devoting much more attention to this topic than the latter.

The first question that needs to be asked is why this topic was included in the syllabus, and why China was selected for examination rather than any of the other socialist countries who may be said to have an 'interest' in Africa?

The answer to the first part of this question lies in the pervasive South Africa preoccupation with 'communism' generally. In 1950 the South African Government passed the Suppression of Communism Act. One does not need to belong to a communist organization to fall foul of this act; it is sufficient to be deemed to have acted in a way that helps to further the aims of communism. Since communism is against apartheid, legal niceties apart, the idea of communism tends to be very broadly construed by the South African official mind and almost any opposition to apartheid tends to be viewed as communist-inspired. This is reflected in the *Official Yearbook of the Republic of South Africa* (South Africa, 1979, p. 59):

While the government initiated as much of its legislative programme related to the Black and Coloured peoples as circumstances permitted, it also had to combat communism which had become a real threat to internal stability.... In 1950 the Suppression of Communism Act was passed making the promotion of communism an offence and excluding communists from trade unions. But legal prohibition of communism did not eliminate it as a threat to the country. It was driven underground and manifested itself, inter alia, in movements launched by the African National Congress (ANC) against the Malan government, and subsequently in attempts at riots and in resistance movements.

Communism is seen not only as an internal threat but as an external one, as shown in the *Official Yearbook* for 1974 (South Africa, 1974, p. 366):

Communism's threat to the security of Southern Africa does not only extend to the support of terrorism against these territories. It also embraces the expansion of influence and the establishment of a presence in all the countries in Southern Africa.... Both the Soviet bloc and the People's Republic of China are supplying military equipment to African states and provide assistance to development projects.

The degree to which official South African concern over communism extends into the education system may be illustrated from a Transvaal Education Department (TED) document relating to a compulsory element of the curriculum called the 'Youth Preparedness Programme', designed for secondary schools. According to Behr, this programme has two components—physical and moral. Physical preparedness is aimed at the acquisition of such skills as firefighting and physical defence in the event of armed conflict. 'Moral preparedness is concerned with cultivating sound moral attitudes and rectitude in the youth of the country' (Behr, 1978, p. 44).

The Transvaal Education Department Circular Minute 134 to schools, dated 30 August 1973, accompanied an 'information guide' on 'Democratic and Totalitarian Government Systems', for the 'Moral Preparedness (Things Worthwhile in Life)' component of the programme. Twenty-five of its thirty pages are devoted to the discussion of communism under the headings 'Communism', 'Karl Marx—Founder of Modern Communism', 'Methods of Spreading the Doctrine of Communism', 'Communism in Practice', 'Dangers for South Africa' and 'Preventing and Combating Communism'. The document opens with a 'Note for the Teacher', which begins: 'No attempt is made to hide the fact that this theme has as its aim the education of our pupils about the evils of communism....'

The 'Curriculum Scheme for Youth Preparedness' lists the objectives of the programme, which range from such things as 'development of an appreciation for the contributions of our heroes' to the cultivation of 'proper relations between boys and girls' and 'the development of positive attitudes toward military duty', and indicates how these might be achieved within the school. It is recommended that some of the programme's aims, such as 'acquisition of knowledge and development of insight with regard to the threat posed to man's spirit by foreign ideologies', should be integrated with the history syllabus. It is suggested that this aim might also be furthered by 'talks on communism, liberalism and other -isms'. Clearly the propagation of anti-communist views is part of official education policy.

The answer to the second part of the question with which we began (why China?) is that at the time that the syllabus was drawn up (1973), China was perceived to be a particular threat. This is borne out by a passage from the *Official Yearbook* of 1974 (South Africa, 1974, p. 367):

The Tanzam railway project, rejected by the West as uneconomic, served as a justification for the introduction of some 30,000 Chinese into Tanzania and Zambia. This facilitated Chinese contact with terrorist organizations which provided admirable fronts for the implementation of their own designs and could also be manipulated to present continued Chinese presence as indispensable to the African cause.

The interpretation of the topic 'China's Interest in Africa' in Joubert (1979) closely follows the official interpretation and more space is given to this topic than any other in the section on Africa. This is apparent from the opening passage of the text (p. 146):

Not only Red [Communist] China but also Nationalist China [Taiwan] has shown great interest in Africa during the past 20 years. By the nature of her communist ideology, it is Red China that constitutes a threat to the Whites of Southern Africa. The emphasis in the following paragraphs is therefore on Red Chinese encroachment in Africa.

The word 'encroachment' reappears throughout the text. To encroach normally means 'to trespass on the rights and possessions of another' (*Everyday English Dictionary*). A map on page 150 of Joubert's book entitled 'Chinese Encroachment in Africa' shows those African countries in which Chinese diplomatic, cultural and economic agreements have been established. South African paranoia about communism allows the normal protocol and trading arrangements undertaken by almost every country in the world to be labelled as 'encroachment' when practised by China. The Chinese are represented as rather underhandedly manipulating an unsuspecting and powerless people, and there is more than a hint of the sinister, inscrutable Chinese misleading the simple, ignorant African as we are told: 'The millions of underdeveloped inhabitants seemed a fertile field to cultivate' (p. 147). Further explanation is in characteristically racial terms: 'China is a non-White country, and for this reason more acceptable [than the USSR or the United States] to the African states' (p. 147).

It is worth noting also that in one of the passages quoted above, China is said to be a threat 'to the Whites of Southern Africa' rather than to the system of white supremacy, just as an earlier quotation referred to the OAU's 'antagonism towards the White people of Southern Africa'. It is characteristic of racist thinking that it should attribute racist motives to opponents of racialism.

The text also points out that the peoples of Africa and the Chinese have much in common in their various development programmes. But once again, Chinese deviousness is implicit when we learn on page 148 that

Chinese projects that have gone no further than the initial stages are shown to visitors from Africa as examples of China's underdevelopment. This reduces the gap between China and the African states and stresses the difference between Africa and the West or Russia.

Finally the text (p. 148) explains that:

It appears that Mao's revolutionary brand of communism has greater appeal in Africa than Russia's more moderate, intellectual brand. Militarism has a strong psychological effect on African leaders, as the military dictatorships of Africa indicate.

Here we have the familiar stereotype of the African as lacking in mental capacity, but warlike.

In Joubert's text, China's interest in Africa is presented in the context of interpower rivalry on the continent or, as it is put, 'the new scramble for Africa'. While the USSR and China are accused of encroachment in Africa, the Western democracies led by the United States are said only to be attempting to halt this encroachment. We are told that 'a desire for world domination became an important reason for Chinese interest in Africa' and that the break in the Sino-Soviet alliance at the end of the 1950s led China to redouble its efforts in Africa, 'being unwilling to leave the field to Russia'. From then on China's task was to 'eliminate both Russian and Western influences on the continent' (p. 147).

In Joubert's text three phases of Chinese 'encroachment' in Africa are identified. The first was a visit to the continent by Zhou Enlai and the establishment of diplomatic relations with a few countries. The second phase involved the support of 'leftist groups', which tried to topple their governments, and what is classified as 'Economic Aid with Ulterior Motives'. We are told that China used economic aid as a means of subjecting the African states to its ideology. The latest phase, according to this account, started in the late 1960s when we are told China gained a stronger hold over Africa by following a policy of 'positive' consultation with African goverments. She also gained admittance into the United Nations. It is this third phase, according to the text, which represents the greatest threat to South Africa.

For apart from increasing its diplomatic ties with Africa, or, as the text puts it, adding to its 'acquisitions', China stepped up its military aid in the form of the training of national armed forces as well as support for 'terrorist organizations' in South Africa's neighbouring countries. A further measure of encroachment is identified in the form of broadcasting to Africa. The text does not mention that South Africa has its own African foreign service, as do many other countries.

Finally, according to the book (p. 152), there is economic encroachment:

It is impossible to give a full account of the Chinese aid programme in Africa; but what is more important are the implications and the ulterior motives that are involved. Neither is it really possible to separate China's political goals from her economic aid. Behind her economic aid there is usually a political motive.

Then we are told that China has used its economic aid as a means of capturing a greater share of the African market. In the United Republic of Tanzania, for example, China has even overtaken and passed the United Kingdom as the major source of imports. It has also managed to conclude many trade agreements with African countries. It seems that from the point of view adopted in this textbook *any* Chinese involvement in Africa is to be deplored because China is a communist country.

The other textbook that deals with this topic, 'China's Interest in Africa', is the one by Boyce (1974*b*). The approach is similar to that adopted in the section on African unity, namely a minimum of text followed by a lengthy journalistic account from the magazine *To the Point* of 10 March 1973. However, unlike the previous account, the article entitled 'New Scramble for Africa' is not included as material for an exercise but as part of the text itself and it is introduced with the recommendation that it is an 'excellent' account.

In the two paragraphs of text that precede the article, we are told that African countries have been dependent on overseas aid from Western countries since receiving their independence. But increasingly, it seems, great alarm has been engendered by the appearance of China on the African scene.

The magazine article follows much the same pattern as that provided in the chapter on the OAU. It is slick, biased and riddled with crude metaphors and stereotypes. It is, moreover, the only account provided. Even more explicitly than in Joubert, the article presents the Chinese as covert, unscrupulous and inscrutable. Indeed the text is positively laced with such descriptions of the Chinese as 'drab', 'unassuming', 'patient', 'secretive', 'coldly calculating', 'invaders', 'a coloured race' . . . the list is long and the stereotype is there. We learn, for example, that China ferries 'thousands of little men into Dar es Salaam, like termites burrowing into the foundations of a building' (p. 205) and that 'they drive a yellow wedge into the Eastern side of Africa'.

They arrive in Dar es Salaam harbour by the hundreds in Chinese ships, all dressed in identical baggy uniforms with peaked caps and wearing Mao badges, looking for all the world like so many automatons of an assembly line. Each picks up a cardboard suitcase—unmarked and exactly like all the others, so the contents must be exactly the same [p. 203].

The account presented in *To the Point* resembles that of Joubert sufficiently closely to make it seem likely that it was used as the source for that text as well. It stresses the superpower rivalry on the continent (called 'beating the Russians'); identifies distinct periods of 'encroachment' (read 'invasion'); and invokes the notion of 'threat'. The Joubert text also makes use of the notion of the Chinese as 'a coloured race' and uses the phrase, 'the new scramble for Africa', the title of the *To the Point* article.

As in Joubert's account, we are led to believe that the Chinese have imposed themselves on the unsuspecting African nations as we read that 'Peking's new approach is also making it increasingly difficult for African states to get rid of the Chinese'. And we are told that there is a strong sense of identification between Chinese and Africans 'because they are a coloured race'.

Again this so-called 'invasion' or 'scramble for Africa' appears in reality to be little more than the establishment of trade, aid and diplomatic agreements. It is, however, the manner in which it is presented that makes this account read like a horror story. The reader is told, for example, that they are 'coldly calculating' in their aid policies (called 'China's Handouts'). Yet the list of the projects and terms of agreement appear no different to those offered by other aid-giving countries whose motives are not questioned either in the article or the main text. The Chinese motives, however, are presented as part of its campaign to become leader of the non-aligned world and to become the dominant influence on the African continent.

There seems no doubt that the hysteria manifested in the article stems from China's support for opposition to white-ruled southern Africa. Thus the author attempts to show that China is using all kinds of pretexts to gain access to the continent. The communist powers are said to be making 'gains' in Africa, while the Western powers 'having no expansionist aims themselves, only react to developments, trying to maintain the status quo' (p. 204).

It seems difficult to understand why such a crude and polarized account should have been selected for inclusion in this chapter, especially since this textbook elsewhere shows signs of attempting to give a balanced account of historical phenomena. It is true that the writing of contemporary history is circumscribed by the availability of up-to-date source material, and journalistic reports may have to be relied upon for information. None the less, even journalistic accounts provide a diversity of opinion, and other interpretations could have been used either to counterbalance this particular one or to provide a less biased account. It would appear that in the context of school textbook preparation in South Africa the quality of scholarly objectivity is prone to evaporate when the question of communism arises. There is no sense in which the sections on China's interest in Africa in either of these textbooks can be said to contribute to the syllabus aim of encouraging the child 'to reason and to think independently' (Aim 3.17, Appendix 5).

Summary

The textbooks' treatment of contemporary African history is broadly in accord with the official South African view of the Black African states. With the partial exception of the book by Boyce the textbooks tend to generalize about African countries from a limited and ethnocentric perspective. Following the syllabus, the textbooks dwell upon the problems in the newly independent states, particularly instances of conflict, military takeovers and one-party systems, and there is a tendency to attribute political and economic difficulties to what is seen as the premature departure of the white man from the continent. Little attention is paid to the consequences of colonialism on either the political or economic development of African territories. Economic development is dealt with within a limited conception of development that neglects the role of international economic relations in perpetuating underdevelopment. Treatment of the Organization of African Unity is ambivalent. The OAU is presented as a threat to white domination in southern Africa but at the same time the textbooks suggest that the organization is ineffective and stress its failures. The treatment of China's interest in Africa amounts to little more than anti-communist propaganda.

8 Conclusions

Our perceptions of the present are conditioned by our understanding of the past. It is this that makes what is taught as history in schools so important. Though history textbooks are only one element in history teaching—and the contribution of the classroom teacher should not be underestimated—they are usually a very important element since they carry the authority of print. In many circumstances, they will be the ultimate source of information about the past for the pupil and, sometimes perhaps, even for the teacher. For very many pupils school history will be the only formal instruction they receive about what went before and what led up to today's world. Beliefs implanted through school history books may therefore persist for a lifetime. History textbooks, probably more than any other kind of school-book, have the capacity to influence the social and political thinking of whole generations, and because of this they deserve scrutiny.

Our main interest in the analysis of South African history textbooks reported here has been in the way they might ultimately contribute to the shaping of public consciousness. Our approach has been sociological, rather than historical or educational. The historian or educationalist might wish to ask different questions from those we have asked about the material we have considered, but we make no claim to specific expertise in these fields. We have sought only to assess how far the pictures of the past offered in the history texts might serve to perpetuate the political and social arrangements of apartheid and white supremacy in South Africa. Are history textbooks to be considered as part of the ideological apparatus that serves to legitimate the present South African social order?

The general conclusion is that on the whole the view of the past offered by the textbooks is consistent with, and frequently actively supportive of, the continuation of present racial policies. There is little doubt that the history syllabus is designed partly with the intention of cultivating attitudes favourable to the maintenance of the system of racial inequality. Textbook authors may or may not share this intention in preparing their texts, but their motivation is not our concern. We have been concerned with the end products, the textbooks, and it is sufficient that these should embody values consistent with official apartheid doctrine for them to be regarded as potentially ideological in their impact.

In some instances this legitimating tendency is quite direct, as when the system of apartheid is described approvingly and the arguments for it directly endorsed. More commonly, however, and perhaps more insidiously, legitimation operates indirectly when the textbooks encourage beliefs, attitudes and values that are part of the intellectual underpinning of the apartheid system or that form part of a world-view into which apartheid fits naturally. It is possible to distinguish a number of characteristic ways in which such ideological tendencies find expression in the textbooks. Some or all of the following are to be found in all of the textbooks we examined in detail. They stem in part from the requirements of the syllabus and in part from the way the history is presented.

Pervasive ethnocentrism. The history is presented very much from a white point of view. This shows itself in the European-centredness of world history in which there is almost total neglect of the history of pre-colonial Africa, of Latin America, and of Asia before the twentieth century. In South African history the textbooks concentrate on the progress of the white groups. Little attention is paid to the concerns of the blacks, who are treated as a problem and an obstacle to the achievement of white objectives.

The glorification of nationalism. Nationalism is a major theme in the history of Europe. The rise of Afrikaner nationalism tends to dominate South African history, occasionally to the point where the English-speaking whites (as distinguished from the British authorities) appear almost as bystanders to the march of events. African nationalism in southern Africa is largely neglected. When it has taken the form of resistance to white domination (for example, the African National Congress) it tends to be suggested that it is misguided and illegitimate, and inspired from outside. Only when it can be presented as tribal loyalty or support for the homeland policy is it favourably commented upon.

The presentation of the past as a model for the present. This occurs most notably in the presentation of racial segregation, the racial division of labour, and the pass laws that enforce these by controlling non-white movement, as normal practices sanctified by time, since they can be traced back to the seventeenth and eighteenth centuries.

Presentation of the historically contingent as natural and inevitable. This is an ideological mechanism closely related to the previous one. By playing down evidence to the contrary and presenting interpretation as fact, the way certain things turned out is made to seem both necessary and desirable. For example, the racial division of labour in South Africa is presented as part of a natural order. Conversely it may be suggested that undesirable consequences flow from attempts to alter the natural state of affairs. For instance, the poverty of the new African states is made to appear a consequence of black majority rule and the departure of the white man.

The perpetuation of myths. There is frequent allusion to the erroneous belief that the Boers occupied an empty land when they trekked north during the nineteenth century, suggesting that this land therefore 'belongs' to the whites. By oversimplifying and ignoring inconvenient facts an exaggerated sense of the solidarity and unity of purpose of the Afrikaners in the past helps to bring the history presented more into line with the mythology of Afrikaner nationalism.

The discrediting of counter-ideologies. All the textbooks that deal with the subject are explicitly anti-communist. This is probably the area in which the textbooks exhibit least 'objectivity' and rationality. Where it is not simply taken for granted that communist ideas are unacceptable, only 'the evils of communism' are stressed. 'Liberal' ideas concerning racial equality are also discredited. Even the French Revolutionary ideals of liberty, equality, and fraternity are treated as suspect and inappropriate in a South African context.

The assumption of black incompetence. There is frequent reference to the idea of non-whites not having reached a sufficiently high 'stage of development', both in the past and in the present, to enjoy full political and civil rights. The extended period of white guidance envisaged for the so-called South African 'black states' before they are granted full independence is explained in these terms. The idea is also exemplified in the textbooks' treatment of the contemporary history of Black Africa, where it is suggested that independence was granted too soon, resulting in present economic and political problems in the new states.

Racism and stereotyping. The idea of black incapacity for government is part of a more general stereotype of the black man as primitive, ignorant, unintellectual and warlike that pervades much of the textbook material. Underlying this is the essentially racist notion of white superiority and black inferiority, and lesser black entitlement by reason of race. While such racism is occasionally explicit it is mostly implicit, finding expression particularly in the sheer emphasis given to the importance of racial ancestry.

In Chapter 3 we put forward four hypotheses. These have served to give direction to the work, and in addition they provide a basis from which textbooks in different countries might be analysed in comparative terms. How do these hypotheses stand up in the light of our findings on South African textbooks? The first hypothesis, that textbooks will tend to support the existing political system of their own country, is quite clearly confirmed. Some of the textbooks give the impression that they have been written specifically in order to lend support to South Africa's political system. The second hypothesis, that dominant groups (in this case the whites) will be more favourably presented than subordinate groups (the non-whites), is also unequivocally confirmed. With partial exceptions it is even true that the politically dominant section of the whites, the Afrikaners, receive the most favourable treatment of all, and the most oppressed of the non-whites, the blacks, the least favourable treatment.

The third hypothesis concerns the question, in the present instance, of whether the blacks are more favourably treated in textbooks prepared for them than in those prepared for whites. This is not fully confirmed. It is true that the Standard 8 textbook written for blacks pays more attention to the history of the blacks than the other books do, and that in this and in the Standard 10 book for blacks passages are to be found that apparently endorse the legitimacy of black aspirations for independence or convey a more positive sense of black identity than is common in the other texts. However, the Standard 10 textbook actually pays less attention to contemporary non-white South African history than the white texts do, and whatever sympathy is evinced for the black desire for self-government is always subject to the proviso that this should be attained within the framework of separate development. In all essentials, the texts for blacks offer no less ideological support for apartheid than those for whites. The third hypothesis is therefore not confirmed by our findings. It is tempting to speculate that where history textbooks serve the function of supporting the status quo in any society the scope for favourable presentation of oppressed groups, even in their 'own' textbooks, is limited by the need (from the point of view of the prevailing power structure) to maintain as far as possible a sense of inferiority among them, or at least an attitude of passive acquiescence to their position.

The fourth hypothesis, that the textbooks' treatment of foreign countries will reflect the home country's historical relations with these other countries

Conclusions

and accord with present foreign policy, is partly confirmed, but ideally more data than we have been able to analyse ought to be considered. The comparative neglect of British history in the syllabus, for example, would seem to reflect Great Britain's past role (in one version of the Afrikaner view at least) as colonial oppressor. The textbooks' treatment of the communist countries accords entirely with South Africa's strong anti-communist stance in international affairs. The image projected of the independent African countries, on the other hand, would appear to derive as much from South Africa's home policy towards Africans as from her foreign policy in Africa.

With regard to our original guiding hypotheses, then, our work on the South African case suggests that the third and fourth hypotheses might profitably be modified and elaborated for use in any future work on history textbooks in other multi-ethnic societies.

Taking the South African textbooks together, the overwhelming impression is that they are better able to serve narrowly conceived white nationalistic purposes than the more academic purposes that they purport to serve. Such aims as 'development of the idea of nationality: the fostering of loyalty, respect and love for the country... love and respect for one's ancestors', etc., in the Transvaal syllabus (Appendix 5) would appear to be furthered at the expense of academic aims such as the fostering of an objective approach to history or the encouragement of independent thought. Not all the books we examined were equally prone to this tendency and it is apparent that not all the authors operate entirely from within the 'white paradigm' of South African history or subscribe to the influential Afrikaner interpretation of history. We have pointed out instances where textbooks have sought to correct common historical misconceptions, to pay more than usual attention to the black point of view, and to present all the relevant evidence impartially on contentious questions. Such practices are, however, the exception rather than the rule, and are generally subservient to the ideological tendencies that we have illustrated. The fact that some of the books do exhibit examples of historical writing against the dominant ideological trend suggests that there is scope for a far less tendentious account of history than is the norm for the textbooks considered overall, even within the constraints of the existing syllabus and the South African education system generally. The key to whatever improvement may be possible under present political circumstances would appear to lie in stricter adherence to the normal disciplines of historical scholarship in the writing of textbooks.

Appendices

Appendices

Appendix 1

Population

Population distribution in provinces and 'black states', 1970 (in thousands)

Region	Population groups				
	Total	Asians	Blacks	Coloureds	Whites
Cape Province	4 294	21	1 385	1 779	1 109
Natal	2 164	523	1 133	68	440
Transvaal	6 579	82	4 338	155	1 904
Orange Free State	1 682	—	1 345	36	301
Subtotal white areas	14 719	627[1]	8 202[1]	2 038	3 753[1]
Subtotal black 'states'	7 175	4	7 138	13	20
Total South Africa	21 894	630	15 340	2 051	3 773
Percentage	100.0	2.9	70.1	9.4	17.2

1. These and similar differences are due to rounding.
Source: South Africa, 1979, p. 26.

Appendix 2

School enrolment

TABLE 1. Enrolment and medium of instruction in white South African secondary schools and the Transvaal, 1978

Medium of instruction	National enrolment (all standards)		Transvaal enrolment (all standards)	
	Number	%	Number	%
Afrikaans	204 231	62.4	117 472	67.7
English	122 543	37.5	55 586	32.1
Other	370	0.1	340	0.2
TOTAL	327 144	100.0	174 398[1]	100.0

1. The Transvaal, according to these figures, accounts for 53 per cent of national white secondary enrolment.
Source: South Africa, 1981.

Appendix 2

TABLE 2. National enrolment in white schools by standard, 1980

Level	Number	%
Substandard A	88 006	9.17
Substandard B	87 212	9.09
Standard 1	88 955	9.27
Standard 2	88 429	9.22
Standard 3	84 871	8.85
Standard 4	82 692	8.62
Standard 5	77 508	8.08
Special classes	9 587	1.00
Auxiliary classes	2 119	0.22
Total primary	609 379	63.53
Standard 6	80 674	8.41
Standard 7	76 794	8.01
Standard 8	73 614	7.67
Standard 9	63 959	6.67
Standard 10	54 696	5.70
Unclassified	127	0.01
Total secondary	349 864	36.47
Grand total	959 864	100.00

Source: SAIRR, 1981, p. 492.

TABLE 3. Black pupil enrolment: primary school, March 1979[1]

Level	White area	Black 'states'	Total	%
Substandard A	308 237	364 188	672 425	22.7
Substandard B	237 400	289 563	526 963	17.8
Standard 1	215 177	273 903	489 080	16.5
Standard 2	163 451	223 253	386 704	13.1
Standard 3	144 823	204 522	349 345	11.8
Standard 4	115 111	160 159	275 270	9.3
Standard 5	107 806	149 272	257 078	8.7
Total primary	1 292 005	1 664 860	2 956 865	100.0
Percentage	43.7	56.3	100.0	

1. Excludes Transkei and Bophuthatswana.
Source: Department of Education and Training, 1980b, pp. 20–1.

TABLE 4. Black pupil enrolment: secondary school, March 1979[1]

Level	White area	Black 'states'	Total	%
Standard 6	76 954	102 893	179 847	35.4
Standard 7	49 188	94 198	143 386	28.2
Standard 8	40 145	84 533	124 678	24.6
Standard 9	13 653	31 163	44 816	8.8
Standard 10	4 088	11 187	15 275	3.0
Total secondary	184 028	323 974	508 002	100.0
Percentage	36.3	63.8	100.0	

1. Excludes Transkei and Bophuthatswana.
Source: Department of Education and Training, 1980b, pp. 20-1.

TABLE 5. Black pupil enrolment: secondary schools in Transvaal, March 1979

Level	Transvaal enrolment	Percentage of total enrolment in white areas
Standard 6	43 362	56.3
Standard 7	29 496	60.0
Standard 8	25 626	63.8
Standard 9	8 350	51.2
Standard 10	2 427	59.4
Total secondary	109 261	59.4

Source: Department of Education and Training, 1980*b*, pp. 20-1.

TABLE 6. National enrolment of coloured children in 1980

Level	Number	%
Substandard A	111 576	14.80
Substandard B	103 220	13.69
Standard 1	98 047	13.01
Standard 2	87 004	11.54
Standard 3	80 186	10.64
Standard 4	70 986	9.42
Standard 5	60 724	8.06
Total primary	611 743	81.16
Standard 6	46 435	6.16
Standard 7	38 702	5.13
Standard 8	24 502	3.25
Standard 9	18 206	2.42
Standard 10	9 303	1.23
Unclassified	5	—
Total secondary	137 153	18.19

Source: SAIRR, 1981, p. 484.

TABLE 7. National enrolment of Indian children in 1980

Level	Number	%
Substandard A	21 907	10.09
Substandard B	23 134	16.65
Standard 1	22 519	10.37
Standard 2	21 352	9.83
Standard 3	20 872	9.61
Standard 4	20 111	9.28
Standard 5	18 700	8.61
Special classes	1 424	0.66
Total primary	150 019	69.08
Standard 6	17 299	7.97
Standard 7	16 401	7.55
Standard 8	15 303	7.05
Standard 9	10 623	4.89
Standard 10	7 525	3.47
Unclassified	—	—
Total secondary	67 151	30.92
Grand total	217 170	100.00

Source: SAIRR, 1981, p. 488.

Appendix 3

Allocation of space to historical facts in South African textbooks

KEY TO THE FOLLOWING TABLES[1]

A: BOYCE, A. N. *Legacy of the Past*[2] (Standards 6, 7 and 8); *Europe and South Africa*,[2] Part 1 (Standard 9) and Part 2 (Standard 10).
B: VAN JAARSVELD, F. A. *New Illustrated History*[2] (Standards 6, 7, 8 and 9).
C: JOUBERT, C. J.; JOOSTE, D. *Geskiedenis vir Standard 6* [History for Standard 6]; *History for Standard 7.*[2]
   JOUBERT, C. J. *History for Standard 8.*[2]
   JOUBERT, C. J.; BRITZ, J. J. *History for Standard 9.*[2]
   JOUBERT, C. J. *History for Standard 10.*[2]
D: PAYNTER, B. E. *Junior Secondary History for Standard 6;*[2] *Junior Secondary History for Standard 7;*[2] *Senior Secondary History for Standard 8.*[2]
E: VAN NIEKERK, A. P., et al. *Ons lewende verlede* [Our Living Past] (Standard 5); *Our Living Past* (Standards 6 and 7).
   SMIT, G. J. J. *History for Standard 8; History for Standard 9.*[2]
   SMIT, G. J. J., et al. *History for Standard 10.*
F: LATEGAN, E. H. *History in Perspective* (Standard 6).
   LATEGAN, E. H., DE KOCK, A. J. *History in Perspective* (Standards 7, 8, 9 and 10).
G: LAMBRECHTS, H. et al. *New History for Standard 5; New History for Standard 6; New History for Standard 7.*
   VAN SCHOOR, M. C. *Senior History* (Standards 8 and 9).
   VAN SCHOOR, M. C., et al. *Senior History* (Standard 10).
H: SYPHUS, E.; CHADWICK, G. A. *Man through the Ages* (Standards 5, 6 and 7).
I: VIVIER, J. M., et al. *Geschiedenis dink-en-leerreeks* [History Think and Learn Series] (Standard 5).
J: VAN RENSBURG, A. J.; SCHOEMAN, J. *Active History*[3] (Standards 8, 9 and 10).
K: MOCKE, H. A.; WALLIS, H. C. *New Structure History*[3] (Standard 8).

1. Full details given in the References (p. 135).
2. Texts approved by the Transvaal Education Department.
3. Texts written for the black education system.

Appendix 3

TABLE 1. Proportion of space allocated to general (G) and South African (SA) history (percentages)

Textbooks	Standard 6		Standard 7		Standard 8		Standard 9		Standard 10	
	G	SA	G	SA	G	SA	G	SA	G	SA
A	49.5	50.5	59.6	40.4	49.9	50.1	48.7	51.3	64.4	35.6
B	48.0	52.0	40.3	59.7	36.6	63.4	39.7	60.3	—	—
C	48.4	51.6	51.2	48.8	41.2	58.8	44.2	55.8	51.1	48.9
D	46.4	53.6	55.9	44.1	37.9	62.1	—	—	—	—
E	49.1	50.9	55.9	44.1	36.9	63.1	52.0	48.0	59.5	40.5
F	49.1	50.9	59.2	40.8	39.6	60.4	38.9	61.1	41.0	59.0
G	48.5	51.5	57.7	42.3	35.7	64.3	50.6	49.4	51.6	48.4
H	45.9	54.1	70.1	29.9	—	—	—	—	—	—
J[1]	—	—	—	—	37.4	62.6	52.5	47.5	53.7	46.3
K[1]	—	—	—	—	35.4	64.6	—	—	—	—

1. Textbooks written for the black education system.

TABLE 2. Proportion of space allocated to topics specified in syllabus: Standard 5 general history (percentages)

Syllabus topic	Textbooks			
	E[1]	G	H	I[1]
Themes from general history up to approximately 1500				
Communications: hieroglyphics; cuneiform writing; origin of the alphabet; Arabian numerals; manuscripts of the Middle Ages; the art of printing	26.6	24.3	21.3	20.4
Agriculture and science: the Egyptians, Sumerians and Babylonians; Greeks; Romans; Arabs; Middle Ages	27.5	20.6	24.9	32.1
The establishment, persecution and growth of the Christian Church	12.6	21.5	20.9	17.1
Industry, trade and travel: medieval trade routes between East and West; the results of the Crusades; Marco Polo; Prince Henry the Navigator; Bartholomew Diaz; Columbus; Vasco da Gama	33.3	33.6	32.8	30.4
TOTAL[2]	100.0	100.0	99.9	100.0

1. These texts contain additional material not specified in the syllabus.
2. Totals in this and the following tables do not add up to exactly 100 per cent due to rounding.

TABLE 3. Proportion of space allocated to topics specified in syllabus: Standard 5 South African history (percentages)

Syllabus topic	Textbooks			
	E	G	H	I
The period up to approximately 1795				
The establishment and development of a European settlement at the Cape up to 1707 by way of introduction	17.1	20.3	19.8	18.8
The period 1707 to 1795				
The population groups at the Cape:				
Officials	2.4	7.6	5.3	7.2
Free burgers	10.4	11.4	3.6	12.6
Non-white groups	10.4	11.8	13.0	11.7
The development of Cape Town	14.6	8.5	15.4	8.5
The trek of the stock-farmers: circumstances leading to the trek; the trek-routes; the way of life of the trek-Boers and the development of a separate identity; contacts with the indigenous population; expansion and settlement	33.0	28.0	23.1	28.3
The last years of the Dutch East India Company and the 'Patriote' movements	12.1	12.3	19.8	13.0
TOTAL	100.0	99.9	100.0	100.0

TABLE 4. Proportion of space allocated to topics specified in syllabus: Standard 6 general history (Transvaal syllabus) (percentages)

Syllabus topic	Textbooks			
	A	B	C	D
Events which contributed to the development of the modern world				
The Renaissance				
Literature	5.7	7.3	6.8	6.6
Art	9.2	10.5	4.9	7.1
Science	7.8	5.8	5.9	4.6
	22.7	25.5[1]	22.2[1]	23.4[1]
Colonization up to 1800	14.9	4.6	14.9	20.2
The Reformation	11.5	23.1	15.5	21.3
The Industrial Revolution	16.8	9.6	12.4	9.1
American independence	18.9	17.1	14.2	12.9
The French Revolution	10.3	10.0	12.7	10.4
and Napoleon	5.0	9.2	8.0	2.8
	15.3	19.2	20.7	13.2
TOTAL	100.1	100.1	99.9	100.1

1. Figure includes additional material not specified in syllabus.

Appendix 3

TABLE 5. Proportion of space allocated to topics specified in syllabus: Standard 6 general history (organized by personalities) (percentages)

Syllabus topic	Textbooks			
	E	F	G	H
Cornerstones of the modern world				
The Renaissance				
Literature	12.9	9.4	5.6	7.7
Art	6.2	5.8	10.3	12.9
Science	10.3	6.5	3.3	9.2
	29.4	25.3[1]	19.2	29.8
Colonization up to 1800	10.3	13.0	13.2	11.5
Most important developments to 1870 as illustrated by a study of historical personalities:				
The Reformation	17.9	20.4	20.2	18.8
The Industrial Revolution	12.5	10.1	14.6	7.3
American independence	12.9	14.3	15.2	21.3
French Revolution				
Robespierre	2.7	8.4	4.0	5.0
Napoleon	6.7	8.4	7.6	5.4
	17.0[1]	16.8	17.5[1]	11.4[1]
TOTAL	100.0	99.9	99.9	100.1

1. Figure includes additional material not specified in syllabus.

TABLE 6. Proportion of space allocated to topics specified in syllabus: Standard 6 South African history (Transvaal syllabus) (percentages)

Syllabus topic	Textbooks			
	A	B	C	D
Introduction: first British occupation; Batavian rule: second occupation	7.6	10.2	2.9	8.1
Most important developments between 1806 and 1902 with special reference to the role of historical figures				
Establishment of Cape as British colony in the time of Somerset	8.2	10.8	13.4	11.2
Great Trek: role of Retief, Dingaan and Pretorius	24.7	19.9	20.1	17.9
Sir George Grey: Bantu policy	4.1	2.4	4.9	3.9
Developments in Transvaal:				
Establishment	4.5	10.0	5.8	5.2
Constitution	15.8	14.0	21.2	14.2
Passive resistance/ First Anglo-Boer War	3.7	8.5	4.6	5.5
President Kruger/	16.5	12.4	11.0	10.5
Second Anglo-Boer War	14.8	11.8	16.0	23.4
TOTAL	99.9	100.0	99.9	99.9

TABLE 7. Proportion of space allocated to topics specified in syllabus: Standard 6 South African history (organized by personalities) (percentages)

Syllabus topic	Textbooks			
	E	F	G	H
First British occupation	3.9	7.4	6.2	7.1
Batavian period and second occupation	3.9	6.8	8.4	6.7
Most important historical developments up to 1902 as illustrated by a study of the role of historical personalities				
Somerset	8.6	10.5	13.7	7.0
Grey	6.0	6.4	11.5	4.5
	14.6	16.9	25.2	12.5[1]
Retief	7.8	7.1	6.9	7.3
Pretorius	9.0	8.1	6.2	5.5
	16.8	15.2	13.1	13.0[1]
Brand	5.6	5.7	6.5	5.7
Kruger	9.9	11.5	7.5	8.1
	15.5	17.2	14.0	14.6[1]
Rhodes	9.0	5.4	3.7	3.4
Molteno	5.2	5.4	—	1.5
Onze Jan	4.3	4.4	5.6	2.3
Burgers	—	—	—	2.3
Steyn	5.6	4.4	4.1	1.8
Sir John Robinson	—	—	—	2.4
Shepstone	—	—	—	3.4
Von François	—	—	—	1.5
Caprivi	—	—	—	0.5
Kreli	5.6	5.7	—	2.6
Chaka	5.6	2.7	3.1	3.2
Mzilikazi	3.9	4.0	3.1	1.5
Dingaan	—	—	—	2.6
Moshesh	—	—	6.5	3.6
Cetewayo	—	—	—	5.8
Maharero	—	—	—	4.2
Witbooi	—	—	—	1.9
Adam Kok	6.0	4.4	6.9	1.5
TOTAL	99.9	99.9	99.9	99.9

1. Figure includes additional material not specified in syllabus.

TABLE 8. Proportion of space allocated to topics specified in syllabus: Standard 7 general history (Transvaal syllabus) (percentages)

General history: Important world events (1815–1961)	Textbooks			
	A	B	C	D
1815-70				
Congress of Vienna	5.7	11.3	4.7	8.1
Garibaldi	5.1	4.6	10.7	5.2
Bismarck	5.5	5.3	10.3	6.8
	16.3	21.2	25.7	20.1
1870-1919				
The scramble for Africa	9.4	12.0	10.7	11.3
The arms race	4.1	1.4	1.9	6.5
Sarajevo and outbreak of First World War	1.8	3.9	2.8	3.9
Lusitania and entry of United States into war	1.8	8.1	2.8	3.2
	17.1	25.4	18.2	32.0[1]
1919-45				
Tension in Europe, Hitler, etc.	21.1	15.5	10.7	12.9
Pearl Harbor	3.9	1.1	1.9	1.3
Capture of Berlin/Hiroshima	6.4	1.4	6.5	2.6
Role of Stalin, Churchill, Roosevelt	1.8	6.7	8.4	3.9
	33.2	24.7	27.5	20.7
1945-60				
Birth of Israel	4.8	9.2	9.3	5.8
Birth of China	10.3	5.3	9.8	9.7
The United Nations	11.5	4.9	9.3	11.6
	33.3[1]	28.9[1]	28.4	27.1
TOTAL	99.9	100.2	99.8	99.9

1. Includes additional material not specified in syllabus.

TABLE 9. Proportion of space allocated to topics specified in syllabus: Standard 7 general history (organized by personalities) (percentages)

General history: The most important developments as illustrated by a study of the role of historical personalities	Textbooks			
	E	F	G	H
The period up to approximately 1918				
Cavour	7.4	6.3	6.5	6.9
Bismarck	9.3	8.1	8.0	8.3
Wilhelm II	3.0	5.1	5.5	4.9
Gladstone	5.2	4.2	5.5	4.4
Disraeli	—	—	—	4.1
Lenin	5.9	6.0	6.5	10.3
Woodrow Wilson	5.7	6.6	7.2	7.4
	36.5	36.3	39.2	46.3
The period up to 1948				
Mussolini	5.6	5.1	5.0	3.7
Hitler	6.3	7.8	5.5	6.5
Stalin	4.8	5.1	5.5	3.4
Churchill	4.8	5.7	4.5	3.7
Roosevelt	6.3	6.0	6.5	4.4
	27.8	29.7	27.0	21.7
The period up to 1960				
Ben Gurion	4.4	6.3	5.2	5.0
Nehru	4.4	4.5	4.7	3.1
Mao Tse-tung	4.8	5.4	5.7	7.5
De Gaulle	4.4	4.2	4.5	3.1
Eisenhower	5.6	4.5	5.5	4.0
Kennedy	—	—	—	3.1
Dag Hammarskjöld	6.7	5.7	5.2	3.5
Adenauer	5.6	3.0	3.2	2.5
	35.9	33.6	34.0	31.8
TOTAL	100.2	99.6	100.2	99.8

TABLE 10. Proportion of space allocated to topics specified in syllabus: Standard 7 South African history (Transvaal syllabus) (percentages)

Syllabus topic	Textbooks			
	A	B	C	D
The most important events (1910–61)				
Unification (role of Smuts and Merriman)	12.2	14.5	13.7	14.7
Period of Gen. Botha (1910–19)	14.2	6.7	6.4	8.6
Period of Gen. Smuts (1919–24)	3.7	6.4	2.4	1.6
Period of Gen. Hertzog (1924–39)	8.5	17.8	7.3	12.7
Period of Gen. Smuts (1939–48)	6.8	7.6	6.4	6.6
Period of Dr Malan (1948–54)	8.1	6.7	8.3	7.0
Period of Strydom (1954–58)	4.8	7.1	3.9	1.6
Period of Dr Verwoerd	3.4	9.7	10.8	13.1
	61.7	76.5	59.2	65.9
How our country is governed				
Legislature, executive, judiciary	0.7	7.1	10.3	32.4
The election, nomination, duties	34.2	14.5	27.0	—
Good citizenship	3.4	1.9	3.4	1.6
	38.3	23.5	40.7	34.0
TOTAL	100.0	100.0	99.9	99.9

Appendix 3

TABLE 11. Proportion of space allocated to topics specified in syllabus: Standard 7 South African history (organized by personalities) (percentages)

South African history: The most important developments as illustrated by a study of the role of historical figures up to 1961	Textbooks			
	E	F	G	H
Two of the following:				
Gen. de Wet	7.5	8.3	6.1	7.3
John Merriman	6.6	3.5	3.7	4.5
Milner	7.5	3.9	5.4	5.9
Emily Hobhouse	6.6	3.9	4.4	4.1
De la Rey	—	—	—	4.5
Gen. Beyers	—	—	—	3.1
C. J. Smythe	—	—	—	1.7
Gandhi	5.6	3.5	3.4	4.1
Escombe	—	—	—	2.8
	33.8	23.1	23.0	38.0
The premiers:				
Botha	9.9	7.4	10.8	6.2
Smuts	8.9	9.2	11.2	10.2
Hertzog	9.4	9.2	13.2	6.9
Malan	8.0	7.0	7.1	4.5
Strydom	4.7	3.5	3.0	2.1
Verwoerd	6.6	12.2	9.5	2.4
	47.5	48.5	54.8	32.3
How our country is governed				
Legislature, executive, judiciary	15.0[1]		21.4	0.3
The election and duties				21.1
Good citizenship	3.8		0.7	2.8
	18.8	28.4	22.1	29.7[2]
TOTAL	100.1	100.0	99.9	100.0

1. No clear distinction between categories.
2. Figure includes additional material not specified in syllabus.

TABLE 12. Proportion of space allocated to topics specified in syllabus: Standard 8 general history

General history: Liberalism and nationalism in Europe to 1848	Textbooks								
	A	B	C	D	E	F	G	J	K
Factors leading to French Revolution	17.7	15.6	22.4	19.8	14.8	17.4	23.7	19.1	22.2
The Revolution in France (1789-95) Meeting of States General, etc. National Assembly/Revolutionary Wars National Convention/Reign of Terror	12.0	19.7	16.6	14.1	19.9	22.1	18.4	21.7	16.9
Napoleon Bonaparte His rise to power Internal reorganization of France Spread of ideas in Europe	38.2	35.3	23.9	28.1	24.4	30.0	28.9	28.9	28.0
Reaction and revolution in Europe (1815-30) Congress of Vienna The Congress system (1815-22)	24.3	13.1	25.9	15.1	17.6	17.4	18.4	17.1	22.6
Liberal and national opposition in Europe February Revolution in France, 1848 Revolution in Germany	7.9	16.3	11.2	22.9	23.3	13.1	10.5	13.2	10.3
TOTAL	100.1	100.0	100.0	100.0	100.0	100.0	99.9	100.0	100.0

Appendix 3

TABLE 3. Proportion of space allocated to topics specified in syllabus: Standard 8 South African history (percentages)

Expansion and partition of southern Africa 1806–54	Textbooks								
	A	B	C	D	E	F	G	J	K
The Cape under British rule									
Introduction	16.0	6.6	7.8	7.6	20.9	15.5	8.8	18.9	14.7
British policy and administration as causes of the Great Trek:									
Forms of government	6.3	4.0	3.1	3.2	5.6	6.9	3.6	4.7	5.9
Hottentots, slaves and Bantu	13.8	13.2	9.9	23.9	10.6	20.7	20.8	5.5	7.7
Immigration	6.6	4.8	5.5	9.5	7.3	8.3	6.6	7.1	5.0
Anglicization	1.9	2.0	1.7	1.0	2.0	0.7	1.5	1.6	3.2
	28.6	24.0	20.2	37.6	25.5	36.6	32.5	18.9	21.8
Southward expansion of southern Bantu									
Migration and dispersal before and after 1806	4.1	5.2	7.2	5.7	4.7	3.4	5.8	6.3	10.8
Mfecane and its consequences	5.3	8.4	4.4	2.6	5.0	2.8	3.3	13.8	10.4
Contact with the whites	6.3	11.6	13.7	4.8	6.6	4.1	6.6	13.4	10.4
	15.7	25.2	25.3	13.1	16.3	10.3	15.7	33.5	41.5[1]
The Great Trek									
Most important trekker parties	10.7	12.2	8.9	15.9	12.6	13.1	12.0	5.6	7.7
White settlement in Natal, Orange Free State, Transvaal	15.7	10.8	28.7 }	} 21.3 {	8.0	9.0	11.7	8.7 }	} 10.8
Sand River and Bloemfontein conventions	13.2	14.6	7.2 }	{ 11.0	15.5	13.1	14.6 }		
	39.6	44.3[1]	46.8[1]	41.7[1]	37.2[1]	37.6	43.1[1]	28.7[1]	22.1[1]
TOTAL	99.9	100.1	100.1	100.0	99.9	100.0	100.1	100.0	100.1

1. Includes additional material not specified in syllabus.

Appendix 3

TABLE 14. Proportion of space allocated to topics specified in syllabus: Standard 9 general history (percentages)

General history (1848–1918)	Textbooks								
	A	B	C	D	E	F	G	J	K
Nationalism and democracy in Europe									
Consequences of Industrial Revolution in Great Britain	19.4	21.8	16.9	—	24.1	25.1	25.4	16.4	—
Unification of Italy	11.0	10.6	9.6	—	10.0	13.7	12.9	10.9	—
Unification of Germany	13.7	11.7	12.7	—	19.5	20.6	16.9	11.6	—
	44.1	50.3[1]	39.2	—	53.6	59.4	55.2	44.4[1]	—
The partition of Africa									
The new imperialism	3.0	6.5	4.5	—	4.3	6.4	4.0	8.4	—
Territories acquired	10.7	9.5	23.5	—	11.4	15.5	15.7	10.6	—
	13.7	16.0	28.0	—	15.7	21.9	19.7	19.0	—
Events leading to First World War									
Triple Alliance and Entente	12.3	10.6	14.5	—	9.8	8.2	10.6	17.0	—
Balkan crisis and outbreak of war	12.0	10.2	4.8	—	7.6	4.6	3.1	6.4	—
Aftermath of war	17.8	10.2	8.4	—	13.3	4.1	8.6	8.4	—
	42.1	33.7[1]	32.8[1]	—	30.7	18.7[1]	25.1[1]	36.7[1]	—
TOTAL	99.9	100.0	100.0	—	100.0	100.0	100.0	100.1	—

1. Includes additional material not specified in syllabus.

TABLE 15. Proportion of space allocated to topics specified in syllabus: Standard 9 South African history (percentages)

South African history (1845–1910)	Textbooks								
	A	B	C	D	E	F	G	J	K
Relations between Great Britain and Boer republics									
Sand River and Bloemfontein conventions	5.2	1.3	1.7	—	8.8	3.8	1.5	2.9	—
OFS, Basuto and British Government	8.6	5.8	5.3	—	7.3	5.5	6.4	8.9	—
Diamond fields dispute	8.6	9.1	11.7	—	5.9	7.3	9.4	10.3	—
Carnarvon's attempt at federation	12.2	17.3	11.2	—	10.3	12.8	15.5	15.3	—
Attempts of ZAR to advance its frontiers	6.5	7.5	10.5	—	11.1	4.1	7.0	7.1	—
Discovery of gold	17.7	19.9	17.2	—	15.0	26.2	18.4	13.5	—
Outbreak of Anglo-Boer War	11.9	8.7	9.1	—	8.5	12.2	7.9	10.0	—
	70.7	70.7[1]	68.0[1]	—	66.9	71.9	66.1	71.2[1]	—
Events leading to Union of South Africa	9.6	16.5	17.2	—	9.1	11.0	12.6	13.5	—
Relations between whites, Bantu and Indians									
Extension of white settlement	9.9	5.1	5.0	—	9.7	4.9	7.9 ⎫	12.8	—
Grey's and Shepstone's policies	7.3	4.3	6.2	—	10.6	8.1	6.4 ⎭		
The Indians	2.6	3.3	3.5	—	3.8	4.1	7.0	2.5	—
	19.8	12.8[1]	14.7	—	24.1	17.1	21.3	15.3	—
TOTAL	100.1	100.0	99.9	—	100.1	100.0	100.0	100.0	—

1. Figure includes additional material not specified in syllabus.

Appendix 3

TABLE 16. Percentages of space allocated to topics specified in syllabus: Standard 10 general history

General history (1919–70)	Textbooks								
	A	B	C	D	E	F	G	J	K
Search for peace and security									
Treaty of Versailles	4.4	—	9.8	—	9.5	9.1	7.7	7.8	—
League of Nations	8.3	—	4.7	—	8.4	6.3	8.0	8.2	—
	12.7	—	14.5	—	19.6[1]	15.4	15.7	16.0	—
The world powers (1919–70)									
Communist Russia	8.0	—	6.4	—	7.8	9.6	11.8	8.0	—
Nazi Germany	4.9	—	8.2	—	8.2	9.4	8.9	7.6	—
Japan	4.4	—	4.4	—	5.3	3.3	5.3	4.4	—
United States of America	4.6	—	4.7	—	6.1	3.3	8.7	4.8	—
	21.9	—	23.7	—	27.4	25.6	34.7	24.8	—
Events leading to Second World War	10.7	—	12.9	—	8.0	9.9	10.9	15.2	—
International relations (1945–70)									
United Nations	3.7	—	4.4	—	6.1	5.5	7.0	8.4	—
Cold War in Europe	9.4	—	8.9	—	11.4	12.4	9.7	5.6	—
Clash of ideologies in the Far East	5.0	—	7.3	—	5.5	6.1	5.6	7.4	—
Middle East	6.2	—	7.7	—	6.7	7.4	3.4	5.2	—
	24.3	—	28.3	—	29.7	31.4	25.7	26.6	—
New Africa north of the Zambezi									
Independence movements and nationalism	24.5	—	4.0	—	4.8	5.5	2.4	8.0	—
Problems in African states	3.6	—	4.2	—	2.7	5.2	6.0	4.0	—
Third World and the OAU	0.7	—	6.0	—	5.3	5.2	4.1	4.8	—
China's interest in Africa	1.4	—	6.4	—	2.5	1.7	0.5	0.6	—
	30.2	—	20.6	—	15.3	17.6	13.0	17.4	—
TOTAL	99.8	—	100.0	—	100.0	99.9	100.0	100.0	—

1. Includes additional material not specified in syllabus.

Appendix 3

TABLE 17. Proportion of space allocated to topics specified in syllabus: Standard 10 South African history (percentages)

South African history (1910–70)	Textbooks								
	A	B	C	D	E	F	G	J	K
Political development									
Rise of political parties	7.5	—	3.2	—	6.8	6.3	5.4	6.5	—
South Africa in First World War	2.8	—	4.4	—	8.2	4.0	3.6	4.6	—
Smuts government	1.3	—	1.5	—	2.3	—	2.8	4.6	—
Pact government	6.0	—	1.7	—	2.8	5.0	4.1	3.2	—
Coalition	4.0	—	3.4	—	6.2	5.0	3.6	8.1	—
	21.6	—	14.2	—	26.3	20.3	19.5	27.0	—
Constitutional development									
Recognition of independence	4.0	—	3.0	—	3.7	3.4	7.7	4.2	—
Political and constitutional	8.3	—	12.7	—	12.7	15.3	9.8	13.4	—
	12.3	—	15.7	—	16.4	18.7	17.5	18.1[1]	—
Economic and social development									
Great Depression	—	—	3.2	—	2.5	3.1	1.6	1.9	—
Poor white problem	2.5	—	2.7	—	1.7	3.6	2.3	2.5	—
Mining and industries	13.1	—	6.5	—	4.5	4.8	4.1	3.2	—
White and non-white labour	4.3	—	1.9	—	0.8	1.5	3.9	1.9	—
Urbanization	1.5	—	5.5	—	4.8	4.4	2.3	4.9	—
	21.4[2]	—	19.8	—	14.3	17.4	14.2	15.0[1]	—
Development of non-white peoples									
Bantu	6.0	—	15.4	—	9.5	12.8	9.8	10.6	—
Indians	4.0	—	8.4	—	5.0	6.7	4.6	3.9	—
Coloureds	5.0	—	6.5	—	5.6	5.7	5.9	4.4	—
	20.1[1]	—	30.3	—	20.1	25.2	20.3	18.9	—
South Africa's external policy									
United Nations	2.0	—	1.9	—	2.8 }	5.7 {	2.6	1.9	—
South West Africa	2.5	—	3.6	—	3.4		4.9	3.9	—
Neighbours	3.0	—	7.4	—	9.3	6.3	12.4	7.6	—
Outward policy	5.8	—	4.8	—	2.0	3.6	2.1	3.7	—
United States	4.0	—	0.6	—	2.3	0.8	0.8	1.4	—
United Kingdom	3.8	—	0.8	—	1.1	1.0	1.3	0.9	—
France	0.8	—	0.6	—	0.6	0.6	0.5	0.5	—
Japan	0.5	—	0.4	—	0.3	0.4	0.3	0.5	—
	24.5[1]	—	20.1	—	23.1[1]	18.4	28.4[1]	20.8[1]	—
TOTAL	99.9	—	100.1	—	100.2	100.0	99.9	99.8	—

1. Includes additional material not specified in syllabus.
2. Distinction between categories in this section not clearly defined.

Appendix 4

National Education Policy Act, No. 39, 1967 (2.1)

The Minister may, after consultation with the Administrators and the council, from time to time determine the general policy which is to be pursued in respect of education in schools (hereinafter called the national education policy), within the framework of the following principles, namely, that:

(a) the education in schools maintained, managed and controlled by a department of State (including a provincial administration) shall have a Christian character, but that the religious conviction of the parents and the pupils shall be respected in regard to religious instruction and religious ceremonies;

(b) education shall have a broad national character;

(c) the mother tongue, if it is English or Afrikaans, shall be the medium of instruction, with gradual equitable adjustment to this principle of any existing practice at variance therewith;

(d) requirements as to compulsory education, and the limits relating to school age, shall be uniform;

(e) education (including books and stationery) shall be provided free of charge in schools maintained, managed and controlled by a department of State (including a provincial administration) to pupils whose parents reside in the Republic or are South African citizens (other than pupils receiving instruction on a part-time basis and apprentices);

(f) education shall be provided in accordance with the ability and aptitude of and interest shown by the pupil, and the needs of the country, and that appropriate guidance shall, with due regard thereto, be furnished to pupils;

(g) co-ordination, on a national basis, of syllabuses, courses and examination standards and research, investigation and planning in the field of education shall be effected, regard being had to the advisability of maintaining such diversity as the circumstances may require;

(h) the parent community be given a place in the education system through parent–teachers' associations, school committees, boards of control or school boards or in any other manner;

(i) consideration shall be given to suggestions and recommendations of the officially recognized teachers' associations when planning for purposes of education; and

(j) conditions of service and salary scales of teachers shall be uniform.

Appendix 5

Aims of the history syllabus as defined by the Transvaal Education Department[1]

The general educational aims to strive at in Standards 8, 9 and 10 are:
3.1 To help the child to understand the [sic] man's existence is meaningful and that he lives in an ordered society.
3.2 To guide the child towards self-criticism and self-understanding in the light of the actions of man in the past.
3.3 To help the child in the development of an [sic] own personality.
3.4 To learn [sic] the child to be responsible for the consequences resulting from decisions made by himself.
3.5 The fostering of firm principles and religious convictions.
3.6 To help the pupil to realize that matters that are of value to his time, such as freedom of worship, political development and independence, were won by previous generations through struggle and sacrifice.
3.7 The broadening of the concept of time, space and reality.
3.8 To show the value of it [sic] that problems must be approached from an historical point of view.
3.9 To educate to an objective approach towards history, fostering the habit of first investigating all relevant facts before passing judgement.
3.10 To obtain an insight into the nature of man and into those things that are eternally part of man, such as strife, intolerance, leadership and discipleship.
3.11 To develop a historical sense, that is the development of an understanding of the influence of events on your land, on your people and on the world in general.
3.12 To educate the child to responsible citizenship:
  Civic development: each child must realize that he is a member of a community, a cultural group, a nation, a party, a church, a state, with duties and privileges;
  Development of the idea of nationality; the fostering of loyalty, respect and love for the country and its people; love and respect for one's ancestors; the elimination of prejudices.
  Cultural development: the building of an understanding of our own traditions, the fostering of respect for our own cultural and spiritual values and for those of other groups.
  Social development: the creation and development of a healthy social disposition towards others.
3.13 Understanding of the world in which we live, and that every community, farm, village, town state, peoples and nation is rooted in the past.

Appendix 5 131

3.14 The development of the imagination and the ability to think in the abstract.
3.15 The broadening of the individual's field of vision.
3.16 The sharpening of critical ability, analytical talent and creative power.
3.17 The child should learn to reason and to think independently.
3.18 The more intensive study of history to lead to deeper and more fundamental criticism of the present day.
3.19 To improve in the appreciation of literature, art, sculpture, architecture and music.
3.20 To learn [sic] the child that the development of civilization is not determined rigidly because man is a being who is at liberty to create freely although there are circumstances and determinants that influence his actions and decisions.
3.21 The philosophical concept of history must be brought home to the child.
3.22 The child should learn that economic, social, scientific and technical changes have an influence on political development.
3.23 The child should be led to understand how the world has changed, how the modern world reached its present state and how it can change in the future.

Special aims to strive at in Standards 8, 9 and 10 are:
3.24 To develop knowledge of the subject
    (a) to acquire knowledge of historical facts;
    (b) the chronological order of events;
    (c) historical terminology, e.g. revolution, coalition, manor, Renaissance;
    (d) the child should be aware of the various forms of historical source material.
3.25 How to study and interpret such sources as speeches, letters, diaries, newspapers, cuttings, government documents, graphic representations, photographs, museum material and books.
3.26 To understand the interrelation between the different world events.
3.27 The child should be able to analyse and synthesize historical material.
3.28 To encourage the child to read newspapers and books; to listen to world news; to develop the sense of curiosity.

---

1. The syntax of this document suggests that it has been translated from Afrikaans.

Appendix 6

Summary of explanations for actions of different groups on the Eastern frontier as given in Van Jaarsveld (1974) and in Boyce (1979)

Van Jaarsveld

BRITISH GOVERNMENT AND AGENTS

Governors adopted a policy of territorial segregation. Changes in frontier policy were partly due to changes in Colonial Office policy. The British Government was influenced by the philanthropists. Policy was constrained by lack of funds and soldiers. Caledon wanted to maintain segregation by settling farmers along the frontier. Somerset sought to put an end to unrest. To keep white and black apart he brought in British settlers. He introduced the spoor system to retrieve stolen cattle. Influenced by the philanthropists, Bourke believed that the white farmers stole Xhosa cattle and he abolished the commando system in order to protect the Xhosa. D'Urban adopted a humanitarian attitude on instructions from London. Glenelg (the Secretary for Colonies), influenced by the philanthropists, rejected D'Urban's frontier settlement and adopted a policy of reconciliation in order to prevent wars.

MISSIONARIES AND PHILANTHROPISTS

They aimed to protect the Xhosa from exploitation. They sided with the Bantu and sought to influence the British Government.

COLONISTS

They needed land for grazing. They were confused by vacillation of government policy, and both British and Boer were discouraged by lack of government protection. Cattle thefts caused unrest and they were disappointed at their loss of land and embittered by Glenelg's policy. The Afrikaners lost confidence in Britain and sought to establish their own independent republics. The British settlers sympathized with them.

XHOSA

They needed land for grazing. They saw vacillation as weakness and were confused. Ndlambe (Gaika's uncle) influenced by Makanna (a witchdoctor) saw Gaika as pro-white because of his meeting with Somerset and so attacked Gaika. When Somerset sent troops to Gaika's assistance Makanna took revenge by attacking Grahamstown. The Xhosa stole cattle.

Boyce

BRITISH GOVERNMENT AND AGENTS

Governors sought a solution to the problem of the frontier. The Bantu were a barrier to the European conquest of South Africa. Somerset favoured a policy of complete segregation, obtained Gaika's agreement to the spoor law, and sent for settlers to strengthen the frontier from Xhosa invasion. Under Philip's influence D'Urban made a treaty with Waterboer (a Griqua chief) and armed him as a means of keeping the peace.

MISSIONARIES AND PHILANTHROPISTS

The missionaries were critical of Somerset's frontier arrangements. Philip feared that the Griquas would be dispossessed by farmers trekking into Transorangia. He believed in territorial segregation to protect the less civilized blacks from competition with the whites and wanted treaties made with the Xhosa as with the Griquas.

COLONISTS

They needed extensive grazing. The spoor law led to abuses and the settlers sometimes took back more cattle than had been stolen from them. They wanted to trade with the Xhosa. The farmers were dismayed and disgusted when not given land as promised by D'Urban and blamed by Glenelg for the Sixth Frontier War. They trekked because they felt there would never be peace and security on the frontier.

XHOSA

Shaka (the Zulu chief) was warlike. His attacks on other tribes caused unrest and the Xhosa were pushed from behind but blocked by the Europeans. They raided the colony. There was intertribal warfare among the Xhosa (no details) and 'an invasion of the colony followed'.

References

AMERICAN COUNCIL ON EDUCATION. 1949. *Intergroup Relations in Teaching Materials: A Survey and Appraisal.* Washington, D.C., American Council on Education.
AUERBACH, F. E. 1965. *The Power of Prejudice in South African Education.* Cape Town, A.A. Balkema.
BEHR, A. L. 1978. *New Perspectives in South African Education.* Durban, Butterworth.
BILLINGTON, R. A. 1966. Bias in History Textbooks. *Education Digest*, Vol. 31, No. 8, p. 37.
BOYCE, A. N. 1973a. *Legacy of the Past, A History for Standard 6.* Cape Town, Juta.
——. 1973b. *Legacy of the Past, A History for Standard 7.* Cape Town, Juta.
——. 1973c. *Legacy of the Past, A History for Standard 8.* Cape Town, Juta.
——. 1974a. *Europe and South Africa: A History for Standard 9.* Cape Town, Juta.
——. 1974b. *Europe and South Africa,* Part 2: *A History for Standard 10.* Cape Town, Juta.
CORNEVIN, M. 1980. *Apartheid: Power and Historical Falsification.* Paris, Unesco.
COSTO, R. (ed.) 1970. *Textbooks and the American Indian.* San Francisco, Indian Historian Press.
DEPARTMENT OF EDUCATION AND TRAINING. 1979. *Annual Report RP101, 1979.* Pretoria, Department of Education and Training.
——. 1980a. *Educamus*, Vol. XXVI, No. 3, April.
——. 1980b. *Educamus*, Vol. XXVI, No. 7, September.
DE VILLIERS, R. 1979. South African Politics: The Rising Tide of Colour. In: E. Hellmann and H. Lever (eds.), *Conflict and Progress: Fifty Years of Race Relations in South Africa.* Johannesburg, Macmillan.
HANCOCK, W. K. 1962. *Smuts*, Vol. 1. Cambridge, Cambridge University Press.
HATCH, S. 1962. Coloured People in School Textbooks. *Race*, Vol. IV, No. 1, p. 64.
HENRY, J. Our Inaccurate Textbooks. *Indian Historian*, Vol. 1, pp. 21-4.
JOUBERT, C. J. 1977. *History for Standard 8.* Johannesburg, Perskor.
——. 1979. *History for Standard 10.* Johannesburg, Perskor.
JOUBERT, C. J.; BRITZ, J. J. 1977. *History for Standard 9.* Johannesburg, Perskor.
JOUBERT, C. J.; JOOSTE, D. 1973. *History for Standard 7.* Johannesburg, Perskor.
——. 1977. *Geskiedenis vir Standard 6.* Johannesburg, Perskor.
LAMBRECHTS, H. A.; SMIT, G. J. J.; VAN SCHOOR, M. C. E. 1979a. *New History for Standard 5.* Goodwood, Nasou.
——. 1979b. *New History for Standard 6.* Goodwood, Nasou.
——. *Nuwe Geskiedenis vir Standard 7.* Goodwood, Nasou.
LATEGAN, E. H. W.; DE KOCK, A. J. 1977. *History in Perspective, Standard 9.* Johannesburg, Perskor.
——. 1978a. *History in Perspective, Standard 6.* Johannesburg, Perskor.

LATEGAN, E. H. W.; DE KOCK, A. J. 1978b. *History in Perspective, Standard 7.* Johannesburg, Perskor.
——. 1978c. *History in Perspective, Standard 10.* Johannesburg, Perskor.
——. 1979. *History in Perspective, Standard 8.* Johannesburg, Perskor.
LAWRENCE, P. 1981. Slap in the Face for South African Education Team. *Guardian*, 12 October.
LEWSEN, P. 1975. Rand Daily Mail Inquiry. *Rand Daily Mail*, 24 September.
MCDIARMID, G.; PRATT, D. 1971. *Teaching Prejudice: A Content Analysis of Social Studies Textbooks Authorized for Use in Ontario.* Ontario Institute for Studies in Education. (Curriculum Series 12.)
MALHERBE, E. G. 1977. *Education in South Africa*, Volume II. Cape Town, Juta.
MARKS, S. 1980. South Africa: 'The Myth of the Empty Land'. *History Today*, Vol. 30, January.
MARKS, S.; ATMORE, A. (eds.). 1980. *Economy and Society in Pre-Industrial South Africa.* London, Longman.
MICHIGAN COMMITTEE REPORTS. 1968. Textbooks Unfair to Minorities. *Michigan Educational Journal*, Vol. 46, pp. 41–2.
MOCKE, H. A.; WALLIS, H. C. *New Structure History, Standard 8.* Goodwood, Via Afrika.
NASH, R. 1972. History as She is Writ. *New Society*, 3 August, pp. 230–2.
NIEVES-FALCON, L. 1980. The Oppressive Function of Values, Concepts and Images in Children's Books. In R. Preiswerk (ed.), *The Slant of the Pen: Racism in Children's Books.* Geneva, World Council of Churches.
NORUWANA, J. M. 1980. *Through the Key-hole: Education in South Africa for the Future.* Paper presented at the Kenton-At-Wilgespruit Conference, Johannesburg, 8 November.
OLIVER, R.; FAGE, J. D. 1970. *A Short History of Africa.* Harmondsworth, Penguin.
PAYNTER, B. E. *Junior Secondary History for Standard 6.* Cape Town, Nasou.
——. *Junior Secondary History for Standard 7.* Cape Town, Nasou.
PAYNTER, B. E.; COETSEE, A. G. *Senior Secondary History for Standard 8.* Cape Town, Nasou.
PODESTA, A.; VAN RENSBURG, A. P. J.; VAN DER MERWE, C. 1976. *Active Social Studies, Standard 7.* Pretoria, De Jager-HAUM.
POOL, I. DE S. 1959. *Trends in Content Analysis.* Urbana, University of Illinois Press.
PREISWERK, R.; PERROT, D. 1978. *Ethnocentrism and History: Africa, Asia and Indian America in Western Textbooks.* New York, NOK.
ROSE, B.; TUNMER, R. 1975. *Documents in South African Education.* Johannesburg, Ad. Donker.
SAIRR (SOUTH AFRICAN INSTITUTE OF RACE RELATIONS). 1979. *Education for a New Era.* Johannesburg, South African Institute of Race Relations.
——. 1981. *Survey of Race Relations in South Africa (1980).* Johannesburg, South African Institute of Race Relations.
SMIT, G. J. J.; KREUSER, F. O. A.; VLOK, A. 1974. *History for Standard 8.* Cape Town, Maskew Miller.
SMIT, G. J. J. 1975. *History for Standard 9.* Cape Town, Maskew Miller.
SMIT, G. J. J.; LINTVELT, H. G. J.; EKSTEIN, T. A.; SMIT, F. P. J. 1976. *History for Standard 10.* Cape Town, Maskew Miller.
SOUTH AFRICA. 1974. *South Africa 1974: Official Yearbook of the Republic of South Africa.* Pretoria, South African Department of Information.
——. 1979. *South Africa 1979: Official Yearbook of the Republic of South Africa.* Johannesburg, Van Rensburg Publications.
——. 1981. *South Africa 1980/81: Official Yearbook of the Republic of South Africa.* Johannesburg, Van Rensburg Publications.
THE STAR. 1975. A Rosy View of Apartheid. *The Star*, 3 April.
SYPHUS, E.; CHADWICK, G. A. 1974. *Man through the Ages, Standard 6.* Pietermaritizburg, Shuter & Shooter.
——. 1979a. *Man through the Ages, Standard 5.* Pietermaritzburg, Shuter & Shooter.
——. 1979b. *Man through the Ages, Standard 7.* Pietermaritzburg, Shuter & Shooter.

TAYLOR, C. 1971. Indoctrination in New History for Schools. *Johannesburg Sunday Times*, 28 February.
UNESCO 1949. *A Handbook for the Improvement of Textbooks and Teaching Materials as Aids to International Understanding*. New York, Columbia University Press.
——. 1963. *Meeting of Experts on the Improvement of Textbooks. Goslar, 14-23 May 1962*. Paris, Unesco. (MAPA/ED/2.)
——. 1974. *Race as News*. Paris, Unesco.
——. 1977. *Ethnicity and the Media*. Paris, Unesco.
UNION OF SOUTH AFRICA. 1951. *Report of the Native Education Commission*.
VAN JAARSVELD, F. A. 1964. *The Afrikaner's Interpretation of South African History*. Cape Town, Simondium.
——. 1974. *New Illustrated History, Standard 8*. Johannesburg, Perskor.
VAN JAARSVELD, F. A.; DREYER, N.; VAN DER MERWE, B. J. 1974. *New Illustrated History, Standard 6*. Johannesburg, Perskor.
VAN JAARSVELD, F. A.; DREYER, N.; VAN DER MERWE, B. J.; KAPP, P. H. 1974. *New Illustrated History, Standard 7*. Johannesburg, Perskor.
VAN JAARSVELD, F. A.; VAN WIJK, T. 1974. *New Illustrated History, Standard 9*. Johannesburg, Perskor.
VAN NIEKERK, A. P.; STANDER, F.; LINTVELT, H. G. J. 1974. *Our Living Past: History for Standard 6*. Cape Town, Maskew Miller.
——. 1975. *Our Living Past: History for Standard 7*. Cape Town, Maskew Miller.
VAN NIEKERK, A. P.; STANDER, F.; VAN ZIJL, A. M. 1973. *Ons Lewende Verlede, Geskiedenis vir Standard 5*. Cape Town, Maskew Miller.
VAN RENSBURG, A. P. J.; SCHOEMAN, J. 1980a. *Active History, Standard 9*. Pretoria, De Jager-HAUM.
——. 1980b. *Active History, Standard 10*. Pretoria, De Jager-HAUM.
VAN RENSBURG, A. P. J.; SCHOEMAN, J.; VORSTER, B. J. 1976. *Active History Standard 8*. Pretoria, De Jager-HAUM.
VAN SCHOOR, M. C. E.; COETSEE, A. G.; LAMBRECHTS, H. A.; OBERHOLSTER, J. J.; PIENAAR, K. J. *Senior History for South African Schools, Standard 8*. Cape Town, Nasou.
——. *Senior History for South African Schools, Standard 9*. Cape Town, Nasou.
——. *Senior History for South African Schools, Standard 10*. Cape Town, Nasou.
VIVIER, J. M.; LOOTS, S. J.; CRONJE, F. J. C. *Geskiedenis Dink-en-Leerreeks Standard 5*. Cape Town, Nasou.
WELSH REPORT. 1936. *Report of the Interdepartmental Committee on Native Education*. Union of South Africa. (U.G. 29-1936.)
WILSON, M.; THOMPSON, L. 1969. *The Oxford History of South Africa*, Vol. I. Oxford, Clarendon Press.

[II40]SS.82/D.162/A